MW00952259

Welcome to the world of home dehydratior preservation that has been used for cent relevant today. This book is designed to guide you through the basics of dehydrating a variety of foods, from fruits and vegetables to meats and herbs. Whether you're a seasoned home cook or just starting, this book will provide you with the knowledge and skills you need to dehydrate food in your own kitchen successfully.

What you'll learn Throughout this book, you'll discover the many benefits of dehydration, including how it can save you money, reduce food spoilage, and provide you with out-of-season flavors all year round. We'll cover the essential equipment you'll need, the best practices for preparing and dehydrating various foods, and how to store your dehydrated goods for maximum longevity.

No part of this cookbook may be reproduced, distributed, or transmitted in any form or by any means, including photocopying, recording, or other electronic or mechanical methods, without the prior written permission of the author, except in the case of brief quotations embodied in critical reviews and certain other noncommercial uses permitted by copyright law.

Legal Notice

This cookbook is intended for educational and informational purposes only. It should not be taken as professional advice. The author and publisher make no representations or warranties regarding the accuracy or completeness of the information and recipes provided and will not be held liable for any errors or omissions. The opinions expressed in this cookbook are those of the author and do not reflect the official policy or position of any agency or organization. Readers should seek professional advice as appropriate.

Contents of the book

Dehydration at Home

Get Started

Before diving into the dehydration process, we'll help you understand the key principles that make dehydration effective. You'll learn about the importance of temperature control, air circulation, and moisture removal in preserving the nutritional content and taste of your food.

Safety First

Food safety is paramount when dehydrating. We'll discuss how to handle food properly, the signs of successful dehydration, and what to look out for to prevent spoilage and contamination.

Creative Uses for Dehydrated Foods

Dehydrated foods aren't just for snacking. We'll explore creative ways to incorporate them into your cooking and baking, adding depth and intensity to your dishes.

In this book, we will focus on using a dehydrator, a device that circulates warm, dry air across food items placed on trays, ensuring even and consistent drying. For those who do not have a dehydrator, a convection oven can also be used, with the same recipes, although it may not be as efficient or economical for larger batches. We'll provide tips on preparing your produce, setting the correct temperatures, and determining drying times.

And a lot more!

By the end of this book, you'll be equipped with the confidence to start dehydrating at home, experimenting with flavors, and enjoying the many advantages of this timeless food preservation technique. Let's embark on this dehydration journey together and unlock the full potential of your home kitchen. Happy dehydrating!

NOTICE

For every food item listed below, we provide essential guidance on selection, preparation, and blanching techniques, complemented by a variety of dehydration recipes. These recipes will detail diverse cutting styles, temperature settings, and duration of dehydration to suit each product. To achieve optimal results in dehydration, it is recommended to integrate these general tips with the specific instructions provided in the recipes. This approach ensures that you harness the full benefits of the dehydration process, preserving the quality and flavor of your foods. Happy dehydrating!

For readers interested in other methods of dehydration or preserving, such as freeze-drying, salt curing, canning, or smoking, we will cover these topics in our upcoming books. There, we will delve into alternative techniques that can be used in different scenarios, providing you with a comprehensive guide to all things dehydration and preserving.

Let's delve into a bit of history!

Dehydration is one of the oldest and most effective methods of food preservation, allowing humans to store food for travel, trade, and longer times. By removing water from food, dehydration the growth of bacteria, yeasts, and molds that would otherwise lead to spoilage. This process not only extends the shelf life of food but also reduces its weight and volume, making it easier to store and transport.

Throughout history, various methods have been employed to dry foods, from sun-drying on hot stones in the open air to smoking over fires. These traditional practices have paved the way for modern dehydration techniques, allowing us to enjoy preserved foods with ease and convenience. The earliest records of dehydration date back to prehistoric times, when our ancestors discovered that dried seeds and nuts could be stored for extended periods. Ancient Egyptians used the hot desert sun to dry fruits and fish, while Native Americans created pemmican by combining dried meat with fat and berries. The Babylonians and Assyrians sun-dried fruits and vegetables on their rooftops, while the Chinese air-dried eggs to extend their usability. In the Middle Ages, dried fish and meats were staples for sailors on long voyages, providing essential nutrients without the risk of spoilage. The Incas of South America used the high altitude and low humidity of their mountainous regions to freeze-dry potatoes, creating a product known as "chuño." During World War II, dehydration technology advanced significantly as a way to supply troops with reliable food sources. Over time, dehydration methods evolved, but the principle remained the same: remove water to extend the life of food. Today, we have sophisticated equipment designed specifically for dehydrating a wide range of foods.

Transitioning from the grand scale of historical and industrial dehydration methods, let's focus on the art of home dehydration. This practice allows individuals to harness the power of preservation within their own kitchens, creating a bridge between the ancient traditions and the modern-day desire for self-sufficiency and healthy living.

The Benefits of Dehydrating at Home

One of the key benefits of home dehydration is the control it gives you over the quality and origin of your food. You can select the freshest produce, perhaps even from your own garden, and dry it without any added preservatives or chemicals. This not only ensures a healthier product but also deepens the connection between you and the food you consume.

A Personal Touch to Preservation

Home dehydration is more than just a method of food preservation; it's a personal journey into the culinary arts. With the availability of user-friendly dehydrators, anyone can dry their favorite fruits, vegetables, herbs, and meats with ease. The process is simple: slice the food into even pieces, arrange them on the dehydrator trays, and let the machine work its magic. The result is a bounty of flavorful, nutrient-rich, and long-lasting snacks and ingredients.

Creative Possibilities

The creative possibilities with home dehydration are endless. You can experiment with making your own fruit leathers, vegetable chips, or herb blends. These homemade treats are perfect for on-the-go snacking, camping trips, or as thoughtful, handmade gifts for friends and family.

Sustainability and Cost-Effectiveness

Dehydrating food at home is also a sustainable choice. It reduces reliance on commercially processed foods, cuts down on packaging waste, and can save money in the long run. By preserving seasonal produce, you can enjoy your favorite flavors year-round, regardless of market prices or availability.

Community and Sharing

Moreover, home dehydration fosters a sense of community. Sharing recipes, techniques, and the fruits of your labor with others can inspire a collective appreciation for this timeless practice. It's a way to pass down knowledge, connect with fellow food enthusiasts, and contribute to a culture of mindful consumption.

Health and Nutrition

Dehydrating food at home allows you to retain most of the nutrients and vitamins present in fresh produce. Unlike some commercial drying processes that may involve high temperatures, home dehydration can be done at lower temperatures, which helps preserve the nutritional content. This means you can enjoy healthy snacks that are free from artificial additives and high in natural goodness.

Tailored to Taste

Home dehydration gives you the freedom to season your food exactly how you like it. Whether you prefer your apple chips with a dash of cinnamon or your beef jerky extra spicy, you can customize the flavors to suit your palate. This personalization makes home-dehydrated foods uniquely satisfying.

Versatility in the Kitchen

Dehydrated ingredients can be used in a variety of recipes, from soups and stews to baked goods and salads. They add depth of flavor and texture to dishes, making them more interesting and enjoyable.

Reduction in Food Waste

By dehydrating surplus produce, you can reduce food waste significantly. Overripe fruits, excess vegetables from the garden, or herbs that are about to wilt can all be given a new lease on life through dehydration.

Emergency Preparedness

Having a stockpile of dehydrated foods ensures that you have access to nutritious meals during emergencies, power outages, or natural disasters. It's a practical way to prepare for unforeseen circumstances.

Altogether, home dehydration is not just about preserving food; it's about preserving a healthy, sustainable, and flavorful way of life. It's a lifestyle choice that promotes health, creativity, and sustainability.

Before we dive deeper into the world of dehydration, let's address some common concerns: **IS IT SAFE? NUTRITIOUS? HEALTHY?**

Since you've acquired this book, it's likely that you already have some understanding of dehydration. However, I'd like to take a moment to emphasize the key points for beginners embarking on their dehydration journey. A common question we receive is whether dehydrated food is safe and healthy to consume. This concern is understandable, as the safety of our food is paramount. Dehydrated foods are not only safe but also retain most of their nutritional value when properly prepared and stored. Dehydrated foods are indeed safe to consume and can maintain a high level of their original nutritional content when the dehydration process is carried out correctly. Here's why:

Safety of Dehydrated Foods:

Microbial Inhibition: The primary factor that makes dehydrated foods safe is the significant reduction of water content. Most bacteria, yeasts, and molds require moisture to grow. By removing water, dehydration effectively inhibits the growth of these microorganisms, which are the common culprits of food spoilage and foodborne illnesses.

Chemical Stability: Dehydration slows down chemical reactions that can lead to food degradation. This includes the oxidation of fats, which can cause rancidity, and the breakdown of vitamins, which can reduce nutritional value.

Long-Term Storage: When stored in airtight containers and kept in cool, dark conditions, dehydrated foods can last for months or even years without significant deterioration, making them a reliable source of nutrition over time.

Nutritional Value Retention:

Vitamin and Mineral Preservation: While some vitamins, particularly vitamin C and some B vitamins, are sensitive to heat and may be partially lost during dehydration, many minerals and fat-soluble vitamins like vitamins A, D, E, and K are well-retained.

Concentration of Nutrients: As water is removed, the nutrients in food become more concentrated. This means that dehydrated foods can provide a more potent source of vitamins, minerals, and fiber per serving compared to their fresh counterparts.

Enzyme Inactivation: Blanching, a common step before dehydrating certain foods, helps inactivate enzymes that can cause undesirable changes in flavor, color, and texture. This also helps preserve the nutritional and sensory qualities of the food.

Ensuring Optimal Nutritional Value:

Proper Preparation: To maximize nutrient retention, it's important to prepare foods quickly after harvesting and to dehydrate them promptly. This reduces the time for nutrient loss to occur.

Controlled Dehydration Conditions: Using the right temperature and time settings for each type of food can help preserve nutrients. Overheating can destroy heat-sensitive nutrients, so following recommended guidelines is key.

Protection from Light and Oxygen: Once dehydrated, foods should be stored in airtight containers that protect them from light and oxygen, both of which can degrade nutrients over time.

By understanding and applying these principles, you can ensure that your dehydrated foods are not only safe to eat, but also nutritionally valuable. It's a fantastic way to enjoy your favorite foods with peace of mind and good health. Happy dehydrating!

Dehydration is more than just a way to keep food from spoiling; it's a culinary tradition that has shaped human history and continues to evolve today. Let's continue our exploration and uncover the full potential of dehydration at home. Happy dehydrating!

Equipment for Dehydration at Home

To start dehydrating food at home, you'll need some essential equipment to ensure a smooth and efficient process. As we prepare to delve into the essentials for this culinary adventure, it's important to equip yourself with the right tools for success. This chapter is dedicated to assembling your home dehydration station with tools that will make the process efficient, enjoyable, and successful. From the indispensable dehydrator to the humble cutting board, each piece of equipment plays a pivotal role in transforming your favorite foods into nutritious, shelf-stable delights.

Dehydrator. How to choose

At the heart of home dehydration is the dehydrator itself, a device designed to remove moisture from food at a low temperature over an extended period. Whether you're a novice or a seasoned pro, selecting a dehydrator that fits your needs is the first step towards creating your own dried fruits, vegetables, herbs, and meats. This chapter is dedicated to understanding the dehydrator, its functions, and how it can be the cornerstone of your food preservation endeavors.

When it comes to **choosing the best dehydrator** for your home, understanding the different types available and their features is crucial. Dehydrators can be broadly categorized into two types: Stackable Tray Dehydrators and Shelf Tray Dehydrators.

Stackable Tray Dehydrators are typically the same as Circular or Round Dehydrators, square shapes are rare. These are the most commonly found dehydrators in stores. They typically feature around 5 trays and have the heater and fan fitted into the lid or the base. The trays have a hole in the center for air circulation. These dehydrators are indeed quite popular due to their affordability and compact size, making them suitable for small kitchens or occasional use. They are a great choice for beginners or those with limited space. It should be kept in mind: Most dehydrator trays are round with a hole in the middle. The hole in the middle and round shape reduces capacity per tray by 20 percent to 45 percent per tray, compared to a square tray with no hole in the middle. While they are compact and may be more affordable, one more downside is that the trays must be rotated during the drying process, as the top and bottom trays tend to dry faster than the others.

Shelf Tray Dehydrators also known as Square or Rectangular Dehydrators: resemble a small oven and have trays that slide in and out, similar to oven racks. This design provides easier access to the food being dehydrated and allows for horizontal airflow, which promotes more uniform drying across all trays without the need to rotate them. The square or rectangular models are often preferred by more serious dehydrating enthusiasts. They are well-suited for larger batches and can handle a wider variety of foods, including thicker cuts of meat or larger fruits and vegetables, or more delicate items that require consistent conditions. These models often come with features like adjustable thermostats, timers, and expandable trays. They tend to be larger and may have a higher price point, but the investment can be worth it for the convenience and quality of the drying process.

Additional Features to Consider:

Timer: A timer can be very handy as it allows you to set the dehydrator to run for a specific amount of time, after which it will shut off automatically.

Materials: Look for dehydrators made from BPA-free plastics or stainless steel for durability and food safety.

Ease of Use: Consider how user-friendly the dehydrator is. Digital controls can offer more precision, while analog dials might be simpler for some users.

Capacity: Think about how much food you plan to dehydrate at one time. If you have a large family or intend to dehydrate in bulk, opt for a dehydrator with more trays or larger capacity.

Temperature Control: Look for a dehydrator that allows you to adjust the temperature settings. Different foods require different drying temperatures, so this feature will give you more flexibility.

Ease of Cleaning: Consider how easy it is to clean the dehydrator. Removable trays that are dishwasher safe can save you a lot of time and effort.

Noise Level: Some dehydrators can be quite noisy. If you plan to run your dehydrator overnight or live in a small space, look for a quieter model.

Warranty: A longer warranty can give you peace of mind. Check the warranty period and what it covers before making your purchase.

When choosing a dehydrator, it's also a good idea to read reviews and compare different models to see which one fits your specific needs and budget. Keep in mind the types of food you plan to dehydrate most often and the quantity you'll be working with. This will help you determine the best dehydrator for your home!

Common question

What to do if your dehydrator is without temperature control?

If your dehydrator does not have temperature control, it may be difficult to dehydrate different foods properly. Most dehydrators without temperature control are set somewhere between 125-165°F, which is suitable for most fruits, vegetables, and meats. However, some foods may require lower or higher temperatures to preserve their quality and safety.

Some of the tips for using a dehydrator without temperature control are:

- Check the food frequently and rotate the trays if needed to ensure even drying.

- Use a thermometer to measure the temperature inside the dehydrator and adjust the airflow accordingly. You can use a fan, a vent, or a window to increase or decrease the air circulation.

- Cut the food into uniform pieces and arrange them in a single layer on the trays, leaving some space between them for airflow.

How can I tell if my dehydrator is working properly?

To verify that your dehydrator is in good condition, you can do these things:

Listen for Noise: Dehydrators usually make a distinct sound when they are on. If you can hear it, then the dehydrator is working.

Measure the Temperature: The best way to check if your dehydrator is doing its job is to measure the internal temperature: Plug in the dehydrator, turn it on, and make sure there is no food inside. Adjust the temperature to your preference and put a thermometer inside. Wait for 10 to 15 minutes for the dehydrator to heat up, then read the thermometer. The machine should reach the set temperature after 15 minutes. A variation of about ten degrees up or down over time is normal.

Inspect the Unit: Look for any signs of damage or wear to the unit. Make sure the trays are whole, and the fan is clear of any blockages.

Test with Food: If you don't have a thermometer, you can do a practical test by dehydrating a small amount of food. Set the dehydrator to the suggested temperature for the food you're testing and see if it dehydrates well within the expected time frame.

Dehydrator Trays

This chapter will introduce you to the various types of trays that play a crucial role in the dehydration process. Each type of tray serves a unique purpose, whether it's accommodating liquid purees, ensuring small herbs don't slip away, or handling sticky fruit leathers. We'll explore the various tray options available, their functionalities, and how to choose the right ones for your dehydrating endeavors. Understanding the differences between non-stick, mesh, and solid trays will empower you to maximize the efficiency of your dehydrator and the quality of your preserved foods. So, let's get ready to dive into the details and set the foundation for your dehydration success.

Non-stick trays are a valuable addition to your dehydrator setup, especially when you're working with sticky or semi-liquid foods like fruit leathers or marinated meats for jerky. These trays are typically made from silicone or Teflon-coated materials, providing a reliable non-stick surface that's safe for food contact. They're designed to be reusable, which is not only cost-effective but also better for the environment compared to single-use alternatives. The ease of cleaning is another benefit, as food residues can be wiped off or rinsed away without hassle. Their versatility extends beyond dehydrators; they can be used as baking mats or liners in various kitchen appliances. Durability is a key feature, with high-quality non-stick trays able to resist high temperatures and withstand regular use. You can find them in different sizes, and they can even be customized by cutting to fit any dehydrator model. When shopping for non-stick trays, it's important to choose BPA-free options that are rated for high temperatures to ensure health safety. Some come with edges or lips to contain liquids, making them particularly useful for liquid-based foods. Incorporating non-stick trays into your dehydrating process enhances the quality of your dried foods and simplifies the overall experience.

Mesh Trays are an integral part of the dehydration process, especially when dealing with smaller food items that could fall through larger gaps. These trays are constructed with a fine mesh material, which provides excellent airflow while preventing small pieces from slipping through during dehydration. The mesh material is typically made from food-safe, durable substances like stainless steel or BPA-free plastics, ensuring that it can withstand the low to moderate temperatures used in dehydrators. The fine mesh design is not only great for small items like herbs, spices, and berries, but it also allows for better air circulation around the food, leading to more even drying. One of the advantages of using Mesh Trays is that they can be easily cleaned and reused, making them a sustainable choice for regular dehydrating activities. They are also versatile, as they can be used for a variety of foods without the need for additional liners or sheets. When selecting Mesh Trays, it's important to choose ones that are compatible with your specific dehydrator model. Some trays are designed to be universal, while others are made for particular brands or models. Additionally, the mesh size can vary, so consider the types of food you'll be dehydrating most often and select a mesh size that will accommodate those items without the risk of them falling through. In summary, Mesh Trays are a practical and efficient choice for dehydrating a wide range of foods, providing the necessary support and airflow to achieve perfectly dried results every time.

Solid Trays, also known as fruit roll sheets or non-mesh trays, are designed for dehydrating liquid or semi-liquid foods without dripping through the tray. They are perfect for making fruit leathers, drying sauces, or any food that starts as a puree or liquid. These trays are typically made from food-safe plastic or silicone and provide a smooth, solid surface. Unlike mesh trays, solid trays prevent smaller particles or liquids from falling through, ensuring that everything stays on the tray during the dehydration process. Solid Trays are easy to clean since they can be simply wiped down or washed in soapy water. Some are even dishwasher-safe for added convenience. They are reusable, which makes them an eco-friendly option for regular use in your dehydrator. When using solid trays, it's important to spread the puree or liquid evenly across the surface to ensure consistent drying. Once the food is dehydrated, it can be easily peeled off the tray due to the non-stick nature of the material. In summary, Solid Trays are an essential accessory for dehydrating a variety of foods that are not suitable for standard mesh trays. They expand the capabilities of your dehydrator, allowing you to create a wider range of dehydrated foods with ease.

Expandable Trays are a feature of some food dehydrators that allow you to increase the drying capacity of your unit. These trays are designed to be added or removed as needed, giving you the flexibility to dehydrate large quantities of food or accommodate bulkier items. The ability to expand your dehydrator can be particularly useful if you have a bountiful harvest from your garden if you're preparing for a large event, or if you simply want to make the most of seasonal produce. With expandable trays, you can dry more food at once, saving time and energy. When considering a dehydrator with expandable trays, it's important to note the maximum number of trays that the dehydrator can handle. Some models may allow you to add a significant number of additional trays, sometimes up to 10 or more, without compromising the quality or efficiency of the drying process. It's also worth mentioning that while expandability is a great feature, it's crucial to ensure that the dehydrator still maintains even airflow and consistent temperature throughout all the trays. This ensures that all the food dries uniformly, regardless of how many trays are in use. In summary, expandable trays offer versatility and convenience for those who need to dehydrate larger volumes of food. They are a feature to look for when choosing a dehydrator that can grow with your needs.

Stainless Steel Trays are favored in food dehydrators for their robustness and ease of maintenance. Crafted from high-grade stainless steel, these trays are impervious to rust and corrosion, assuring longevity even with frequent use. They're capable of enduring high temperatures and can be spotless, including in a dishwasher or with steam, without any damage. The sturdiness of stainless steel means it won't warp or degrade over time, and its non-reactive nature ensures that no chemicals leach into your food, making it a safe choice for dehydrating. The trays' good heat conductivity aids in uniform drying, and their sleek, professional appearance can enhance the look of your kitchen. When selecting stainless steel trays, make sure they fit your dehydrator model. Some dehydrators include these trays, while for others, they might be an additional purchase. Investing in Stainless Steel Trays is wise for regular dehydrators seeking reliable, durable equipment for their food preservation endeavors.

Additional Equipment for Home Dehydration

Sharp Knives and Cutting Board The foundation of food preparation begins with sharp knives and a sturdy cutting board. These tools are indispensable for slicing your food into uniform pieces, which is crucial for even drying. A sharp knife ensures clean cuts without bruising the food, while a good cutting board provides a stable surface for safe chopping.

Mandolin Slicer For those seeking precision and speed, the mandolin slicer is a game-changer. It allows you to slice fruits and vegetables to a consistent thickness quickly, which is vital for uniform dehydration. With adjustable settings, you can achieve the perfect slice every time.

Blender or Food Processor When it comes to making purees for fruit leathers or finely chopping herbs, a blender or food processor is your best ally.

Non-Stick Dehydrator Sheets or Silicone Mats Dealing with sticky or semi-liquid items is a breeze with non-stick dehydrator sheets or silicone mats. They prevent food from adhering to the trays, making cleanup effortless.

Airtight Containers or Vacuum Sealer after dehydration, preserving the freshness of your goods is paramount. Airtight containers or a vacuum sealer extend the shelf life of your dehydrated foods by keeping air and moisture at bay, ensuring your efforts last longer.

Salad Spinner A salad spinner is not just for salads; it's also perfect for drying washed herbs or leafy greens before dehydration. By removing excess water, you ensure a more efficient drying process and prevent mold growth.

Large Pot for Blanching Some foods, particularly certain vegetables, benefit from blanching before dehydration.

Thermometer and Hygrometer Storing your dehydrated foods in the right conditions is essential. A thermometer and hygrometer help you monitor the temperature and humidity of your storage area, maintaining the ideal environment for your dehydrated goods.

Specialty Tools Time is precious, and specialty tools like cherry pitters, apple cores, and peelers can expedite the preparation process. These tools are especially useful when processing large batches, saving you time and effort.

Overview of the Dehydration Process

Selection: When preparing food for dehydration, the process begins with the careful selection of quality produce. It's essential to choose fruits and vegetables that are not only fresh and ripe but also free from any visible bruises or blemishes. The freshness of the produce directly impacts the flavor and nutritional value of the dehydrated product. Seasonal produce is often recommended as it tends to be at its peak in both taste and nutrients. For those who prefer to avoid pesticides and chemicals, organic options are available and can be a healthier choice.

Preparation: Once the selection is made, the next crucial step is cleaning and sanitizing the produce. This involves thoroughly washing all items under running water to remove any dirt, dust, or other contaminants that may be present on the surface. After sanitizing, it's important to dry the produce completely. This can be done by patting it dry with clean towels or using a salad spinner to ensure that excess moisture is removed.

The **final** step before the actual dehydration process is the pre-treatment of the produce. This can involve several methods, depending on the type of food being prepared. Blanching, for example, is a quick boiling process used primarily for vegetables. It not only enhances the color of the produce but also helps to reduce spoilage and eliminate bacteria that might be present. For light-colored fruits, a lemon water treatment might be applied to prevent discoloration during the dehydration process. To prevent browning and maintain the fruit's color and nutrition, you can pre-treat the fruit. Common methods include using a lemon juice dip or a citric acid bath. For example, you can use 1 cup of lemon or lime juice to 1 quart of water, or spray the fruit with straight juice from a spray bottle.

By following these steps, one ensures that the food is not only safe to consume but also of the highest quality. The dehydration process, when done correctly, can preserve the produce and provide a convenient and long-lasting food supply. Always remember to adhere to food safety guidelines and adjust pre-treatment methods to suit the specific requirements of the produce you are working with. This careful preparation will result in a superior dehydrated product that retains much of its original flavor and nutritional content.

Temperature Guidelines

While it is important to stay within these ranges to ensure food safety and quality, slight deviations may be necessary based on individual dehydrator performance and environmental factors. Always monitor the dehydration process and adjust as needed, keeping in mind that these guidelines serve as a helpful starting point rather than an unyielding decree. This introduction sets the stage for understanding the temperature guidelines as helpful advice that should be tailored to each unique dehydration scenario.

Bread: 135°F to 155°F (57°C to 68°C) - This range is suitable for dehydrating bread to achieve a crumbly and dry texture while preserving its flavor. It's important to use non-oily bread for long-term storage, as oily bread may go rancid quickly after heating.

Herbs: 85°F to 105°F (29°C to 40°C) - This range is gentle enough to dry herbs while preserving their aromatic and medicinal properties.

Vegetables: 115°F to 135°F (46°C to 57°C) - A moderate range that effectively dries vegetables while retaining their nutritional value and color.

Beans and Lentils: 115°F to 135°F (46°C to 57°C) - Like vegetables, this range ensures that beans and lentils are dried thoroughly without affecting their texture.

Fruit: 125°F to 145°F (51°C to 62°C) - A slightly higher range to remove moisture from fruits while maintaining their natural sugars and vitamins.

Grains: 135°F to 155°F (57°C to 68°C) - Grains need a bit more heat to ensure all moisture is removed, preventing mold and spoilage.

Meat: After heating meat to 160 °F (71°C) and poultry to 165 °F (74°C), maintain a constant dehydrator temperature of 130 to 145 °F (54 TO 62 °C) during the drying process.

Seafood, Shellfish: 125°F (52°C) 145°F (63°C) The final product should be brittle or dry-leathery.

Cheese: Should be dehydrated at 125°F (52°C) 145°F (63°C)

Fruit & Vegetable leather: 130°F (54°C) 140°F (60°C). The final product should be pliable and leathery.

Fish: 135°F to 165°F (57°C to 74°C) - This range is ideal for dehydrating fish, ensuring that it dries thoroughly while preserving its nutritional content and flavor. It's high enough to eliminate any harmful bacteria, especially in raw fish, making it safe for consumption.

In the world of food dehydration, precision is key, yet flexibility remains essential. The temperature guidelines provided are not rigid rules, but rather a spectrum within which one can operate to achieve optimal results. These ranges are designed to accommodate the varying sensitivities of different foods, from the robustness of meats to the delicacy of herbs. These temperature ranges provide flexibility while ensuring the safety and quality of the dehydrated foods. It's important to check the specific requirements for each type of food and adjust the temperature accordingly within these ranges for optimal results.

Time Management

Time management is a crucial aspect of the food dehydration process, as it determines the quality and safety of the final product. Here's a more detailed look at time management in food dehydration:

Understanding Dehydration Time The time it takes to dehydrate food can vary greatly depending on several factors:

Thickness of Slices The size and thickness of the food slices are directly proportional to the dehydration time. Thicker slices have more moisture and thus require a longer period to dry completely. Uniform slicing is crucial for even drying, as it ensures that all pieces reach the desired level of dehydration at the same time.

Dehydrator Efficiency The design and technology of the dehydrator can significantly affect the time it takes to dry food. Models equipped with features like Converge-Flow patented technology can circulate air more efficiently, leading to quicker dehydration times. Conversely, less advanced models may require more time to achieve the same level of dryness.

Environmental Conditions Ambient humidity and temperature are external factors that can influence dehydration time. In environments with high humidity, the air is already saturated with moisture, making it harder for the dehydrator to remove water from the food. On the other hand, a dry and warm environment can expedite the dehydration process.

Water Content and Acidity The water activity, which is the amount of water available in food for bacterial growth, is a target for dehydration. Lowering the water activity through dehydration inhibits bacterial growth and prolongs shelf life. The acidity or pH level of the food can also affect dehydration times, as foods with higher acidity levels typically require less time to dry1.

Additional Considerations Other factors that may affect dehydration time include the quantity of food being dried, the dehydrator's capacity, and the specific settings used. It's important to consult the dehydrator's manual for recommended times and temperatures for different foods and to adjust based on your observations during the process.

General Time Guidelines

The general time guidelines for dehydrating various types of food are as follows:

Fruits: The dehydration time for fruits can range from 6 to 36 hours. This wide range accounts for the varying levels of moisture and sugar content found in different fruits. For instance, thinly sliced apples may take less time compared to plump berries or slices of mango.

Vegetables: Vegetables typically require 6 to 12 hours to dehydrate. The time needed can depend on the vegetable's water content and how it's prepared - sliced, diced, or shredded. Leafy greens may dehydrate faster than denser vegetables like carrots or potatoes.

Meats: Dehydrating meats can take up to 24 hours, particularly for thicker cuts or meats with higher moisture content. It's crucial to ensure meats are dehydrated thoroughly to prevent bacterial growth. Jerky, for example, needs to be dried until it is leathery and chewy.

Fish: Fish should be precooked before dehydrating to ensure food safety. It typically requires 6 to 16 hours to dehydrate.

Seafood, Shellfish: From 8 to 12 hours, or until it is dry and leathery. Shellfish such as shrimp, lobster, and crab are low in fat and can be dried, but they must also be precooked before drying.

Beans and Lentils: 8 to 12 hours, or until they are hard and dry. They should not be soft or squishy.

Grains: From 6 to 10 hours. Grains that dehydrate faster are those that are cooked just shy of al dente. Grains that are larger, denser, or starchier may take longer to dehydrate, such as wheat and corn.

Bread: From 1 to 6 hours. The time it takes to dehydrate bread depends on the type and thickness of the bread, as well as the temperature.

Cheese: From 6 to 24 hours. The time it takes to dehydrate cheese depends on the type and moisture content of the cheese.

Fruit & Vegetable leather: 6 to 10 hours, or until it is dry and leathery. The drying time may vary depending on the moisture content of the puree and the humidity of the environment.

Herbs: Herbs generally take the least amount of time to dehydrate, usually around 1 to 8 hours. Because of their low moisture content and delicate nature, herbs can dry quickly and should be monitored closely to preserve their flavor and aroma.

As you utilize these guidelines, remember that they are not rigid rules but rather flexible recommendations. The true essence of successful dehydration lies in the art of observation and the willingness to adjust. Trust your senses, and don't hesitate to extend or reduce drying times to achieve the perfect texture and flavor. Regular monitoring and adjusting based on the food's drying progress are key to successful dehydration.

Monitoring & Testing

Effective monitoring is a critical component of the dehydration process, ensuring that food reaches the optimal level of dryness without being subjected to excessive or insufficient dehydration. To begin with, the type of food undergoing dehydration plays a significant role in determining the duration of the drying process. Variations in moisture content among different food items, such as the rapid drying of leafy greens compared to the more moisture-rich meaty tomatoes, necessitate adjustments in drying times. Furthermore, achieving uniformity in slice thickness is paramount for even dehydration. Disparities in thickness can lead to varying drying durations, with thicker slices requiring a longer period to dehydrate than their thinner counterparts. Therefore, regular inspection of slices of different thicknesses is crucial throughout the dehydration process. Test by cooling a piece for a few minutes and then bending it, usually it should not feel sticky or moist. You will find more details on how to check the food for doneness in the following sections of the recipes, taking into account the unique attributes inherent to each product. Additionally, for those utilizing a dehydrator with multiple trays, it is advisable to rotate the trays at intervals to promote uniform drying, as temperature variations may occur at different heights within the appliance.

By diligently observing these critical factors and consistently monitoring the dehydration progress, one can achieve perfectly dehydrated food that is both safe for storage and delightful to consume.

Post-Dehydration Handling

Conditioning

Conditioning is a vital step in the preservation of dehydrated foods. After the initial dehydration phase, it is essential to allow the food to rest within a sealed container for several days. This resting period serves to equilibrate the moisture content, ensuring that any residual moisture is uniformly distributed throughout the food. This process not only enhances the consistency in dryness and texture but also mitigates the risk of microbial growth that can occur in pockets of higher moisture.

Essential steps in the conditioning process

1. Transfer the Dehydrated Food: Immediately after the dehydration process, transfer the food to an airtight container. This can be a glass jar or a plastic storage container with a tight-fitting lid.

2. Resting Period: Allow the food to rest in the container for 4-7 days. This duration is crucial for the equalization of moisture content across all pieces.

3. Daily Checks: Each day, inspect the container for any signs of condensation or moisture buildup. If you notice any droplets or dampness, remove the food and return it to the dehydrator for additional drying time.

4. Stirring or Shaking: Daily, gently stir or shake the contents of the container to promote even moisture distribution. This helps prevent clumping and ensures that all pieces are conditioned uniformly.

5. Final Inspection: At the end of the conditioning period, perform a thorough inspection of the food. Check for any remaining stickiness, moisture, or inconsistency in texture. If the food has not reached the desired dryness, extend the conditioning period by a few more days, checking daily.

By following these steps and allowing sufficient time for conditioning, you'll ensure that your dehydrated foods are evenly dried and ready for long-term storage. Remember, the key to successful conditioning is patience and regular monitoring. Happy dehydrating!

Storage

When storing dehydrated food, the choice of container and the storage environment play pivotal roles in preserving the quality and extending the shelf life of the food. Opting for airtight containers is crucial as they prevent the ingress of moisture and air, which can lead to spoilage. Glass jars with rubber-sealed lids or heavy-duty plastic containers with snap-on lids are excellent choices for this purpose.

The storage location should be a cool, dark place, such as a pantry or cupboard, away from direct sunlight and heat sources. These conditions help to maintain the food's texture, flavor, and nutritional value. Basements or cellars can also be ideal storage areas, provided they are dry and well-ventilated.

Incorporating oxygen absorbers into the containers can significantly reduce the amount of oxygen, thereby inhibiting the growth of aerobic bacteria and fungi. For those looking to store dehydrated foods for an extended period, vacuum sealing is an effective method. It removes air from the container, creating a near-perfect preservation environment. When stored in airtight packaging with oxygen absorbers and kept in a cool place, some dehydrated foods can last between 5 and 10 years. It's important to note that dried fruits generally have a longer shelf life than dried vegetables, while dehydrated meats are known to spoil the fastest.

Keep in mind, the general shelf life of dehydrated food that has been prepared with oil can be shorter compared to dehydrated food without oil. This is because oils can become rancid over time, which can affect the taste and safety of the food. Typically, dehydrated foods with oil should be consumed within 6 to 12 months for optimal quality.

A few additional tips for ensuring the longevity of your dehydrated foods include labeling the containers with the date of dehydration and the type of food. This practice helps in tracking the age of the stored items and in using older stocks first. It's also beneficial to check the stored food periodically for any signs of spoilage or moisture and to consume it within the recommended time frame to enjoy its best quality.

Vegetables

Storing dehydrated vegetables in a cool, dark place is important. You can use any airtight container, such as glass jars, plastic containers, or vacuum-sealed bags. This will prevent moisture, heat, and light from affecting the quality of the vegetables. These factors can cause oxidation, bacteria growth, and nutrient loss. If you want to extend their shelf life even more, you can refrigerate or freeze them. This is especially recommended for people who live in humid climates or do not have air conditioning. However, you should always check for signs of spoilage, such as mold, discoloration, or bad smell. If you see any condensation inside the container, you need to dry the vegetables again.

The duration of dehydrated vegetables depends on several factors, such as the type of vegetable, the method of drying, the quality of the container, and the storage conditions. However, some general estimates are that dehydrated vegetables can last up to 12 months at room temperature, up to 5 in the refrigerator, and 25 years to indefinitely if vacuum sealed and stored in a freezer.

Fruits

Dehydrated fruit can last from 4 to 12 months, 2 to 5 years in the fridge, and indefinitely in the freezer. However, these are only general guidelines, and the actual shelf life of dehydrated fruit may vary depending on the type of fruit, the drying method, the storage container, and the storage temperature. However, the quality and nutritional value of the fruit may degrade over time, especially in warm temperatures. **To store dehydrated fruit long term, you need to follow some steps, such as:**

- Use airtight or vacuum-sealed containers for storage.
- Pack the fruit as tightly as possible without damaging it.
- Store the containers in a dark, dry, cool place.
- Store the fruit in quantities that are likely to be used all at once.
- Monitor the fruit regularly for signs of spoilage, such as mold, insects, or bad smell.

Fish

There are different ways to store dehydrated fish, depending on how long you want to keep it and what kind of fish you have. Here are some general guidelines:

- For low-fat fish, such as cod, haddock, or halibut, you can store them in an airtight container at room temperature for up to 3 months.

- For medium-fat fish, such as salmon, trout, or tuna, you can store them in an airtight container in the refrigerator for up to 1 month.

- For high-fat fish, such as mackerel, herring, or sardines, you should store them in a freezer bag in the freezer for up to 6 months. Storing high-fat fish without using a freezer is not recommended, as they have a shorter shelf life and are more prone to spoilage. However, if you have no other option, you can store the fish in an airtight container and use it within one or two days.

To prevent the fish from absorbing moisture or being exposed to oxygen, you should wrap them in several layers of paper or plastic before putting them in the container or bag. You can also vacuum-seal the fish or use glass jars with tight lids to extend their shelf life. If you have a cool, dark, and windy place, such as a basement, you can hang the fish on wooden trellises or hooks after wrapping them on paper. You should check the fish regularly for signs of spoilage, such as mold, insects, or bad smell.

Meat

Properly dehydrated meat can last up to six months or longer if dried and stored well. However, it may lose its taste and flavor after three months unless stored in a freezer or refrigerator. Home-dried jerky can be stored for 1 to 2 months, but it should be kept in the freezer for long-term storage because it contains a high amount of fat.

The best way to store dehydrated meat and jerky is to use airtight containers, such as glass jars or food-grade plastic containers, that can keep out moisture and air. These containers can protect the jerky from spoilage and preserve its freshness and flavor for up to six months or longer. Alternatively, you can also use zip-lock bags or vacuum-sealed bags, but make sure to squeeze out as much air as possible before sealing them. These bags can also prevent bacterial growth and oxidation, but they may not be as durable or effective as containers. If you want to extend the shelf life of your jerky even further, you can freeze it in freezer bags or containers. Freezing can keep your jerky safe for up to a year or more, but be aware that it may affect the texture and taste of your jerky after thawing. No matter which method you choose, you should always store your jerky in a cool and dark place, away from heat, light, and humidity. You should also check your jerky for signs of spoilage, such as mold, discoloration, or bad smell, before consuming it. Eating spoiled jerky can cause food poisoning or other illnesses.

Seafood, Shellfish

Dehydrated seafood and shellfish should be placed into zip-lock bags, glass jars, or vacuum-sealed containers. They should be stored in a dark area at room temperature for no more than two months. Dehydrated seafood and shellfish can also be frozen to extend their shelf life for up to a year or more. However, freezing may affect the texture and taste of the food after thawing. You should check it for signs of spoilage, such as mold, discoloration, or bad smell, before consuming.

Beans and Lentils

The best way to store dehydrated beans and lentils is to use airtight containers that can keep out moisture and air. These containers can protect the beans and lentils from spoilage and preserve their freshness and flavor for up to one year. You can also add oxygen absorbers in the earth to your containers for extra protection against insects and mold3. You should store your containers in a cool, dark, and dry place, away from heat, light, and humidity. You should also check your beans and lentils for signs of spoilage, such as mold, discoloration, or bad smell, before consuming them.

Grains

The best way to store dehydrated grains is to use airtight containers with secure lids or closures. You can choose any material that suits your preference, such as glass, plastic, or aluminum canisters, or even zip-top plastic bags. The important thing is to make sure that the container provides an airtight seal that prevents oxygen, moisture, and pests from entering.

You should also store the dehydrated grains in a cool, dark place, away from direct sunlight, heat sources, and humidity. These factors can cause oxidation, bacteria growth, and nutrient loss in the grains. If you live in a humid climate or do not have air conditioning, you may want to refrigerate or freeze the dehydrated grains to extend their shelf life.

The shelf life of dehydrated grains depends on several factors, such as the type of grain, the method of drying, the quality of the container, and the storage conditions. Dehydrated grains can last up to 6 months at room temperature, up to a year in the refrigerator, and up to 25 years if vacuum-sealed and stored in a freezer.

Cheese

The best way to store dehydrated cheese is to let it cool completely before packaging it in an airtight container or vacuum-sealed bag. Then, store it in a cool, dry place away from light and moisture. This can extend the shelf life of the dehydrated cheese for several months to a year.

Fruit & Vegetable leather

The best way to store dehydrated fruit and vegetable leather is to roll them up and wrap them in plastic wrap or wax paper. Then, place them in an airtight container, such as a glass jar, a plastic bag, or a metal canister. Make sure that the container has a tight seal that keeps out oxygen, moisture, and pests. You should also store the dehydrated fruit and vegetable leather in a cool, dark, and dry place, away from direct sunlight, heat sources, and humidity. These factors can cause oxidation, bacteria growth, and nutrient loss in the leather.

The shelf life of dehydrated fruit and vegetable leather depends on several factors, such as the type of fruit or vegetable, the ingredients, the method of drying, the quality of the container, and the storage conditions. However, some general estimates are, that dehydrated fruit and vegetable leather can last up to 1 month at room temperature, up to 6 months in the refrigerator, and up to 1 year in the freezer.

Tea blends

Dehydrated tea blends need to be protected from heat, air, and moisture, which can affect their quality and freshness. The best way to store dehydrated tea blends is to use airtight containers with secure lids or closures. You can choose any material that suits your preference, such as glass, plastic, or aluminum canisters, or even zip-top plastic bags. The important thing is to make sure that the container provides an airtight seal that prevents oxygen, moisture, and pests from entering. You should also store the dehydrated tea blends in a cool, dark place, away from direct sunlight, heat sources, and humidity. These factors can cause oxidation, bacteria growth, and nutrient loss in the tea blends. If you live in a humid climate or do not have air conditioning, you may want to refrigerate or freeze the dehydrated tea blends to extend their shelf life.

Bread

Dehydrated bread can last for 6–9 months in an airtight container, but you should check it often for rancidity.

Herbs

To store dried herbs properly, you need to protect them from air, light, heat, and moisture. You can do this by keeping them in airtight containers made of glass or metal and placing them in a cool, dark, and dry place. It is also better to store them in the largest form possible, such as whole leaves, seeds, or roots, and grind them as needed. Don't forget to label your containers with the name and date of drying and use them within a year for the best flavor and quality. Dried herbs can last from 8 months to 4 years, but you should check it.

Rehydration Techniques

Rehydrating food that has been dehydrated in a dehydrator involves introducing the food to a liquid to restore its moisture content. Here are some techniques you can use:

Boiling Water Method: Boil water and pour it over the dehydrated food. Allow it to sit for 20–45 minutes. Less dense foods like mushrooms will need more time than something like corn. This method also works for fruits, and you can even use fruit juice to rehydrate if you prefer.

Overnight Soak: Fill a container with the dehydrated food and cover it with water, adding an extra inch or two above the food. The food will absorb the water overnight, and you can use the leftover water as part of the liquid in your meal preparation.

Simmering: Add your dehydrated vegetables directly into a simmering soup or stew. This method is convenient as it rehydrates the food while cooking and doesn't require additional dishes.

Remember, dehydrated food is usually not fully cooked before drying, so after rehydrating, it will still need time to cook through unless it was fully cooked before dehydration. Avoid just tossing vegetables into a soup and serving immediately after they've plumped up; they may still be tough and require further cooking time to soften.

**Here are some additional ideas
for rehydrating dehydrated food:**

Steam Rehydration: You can use a steamer to rehydrate vegetables. Place the dehydrated food in the steamer basket and cover it with a lid. The steam will gently rehydrate the food without making it too soggy.

Cold Water Soak: For foods that might become too soft with hot water, such as certain fruits, you can soak them in cold water. This process takes longer, usually a few hours or overnight, but it helps to maintain the texture of the food.

Using Broth or Stock: Instead of water, you can use chicken, beef, or vegetable broth to rehydrate your food. This will add extra flavor to the food, making it more savory and rich.

Milk Soak for Cereals and Grains: If you're rehydrating cereals or grains like oats or wheat, you can soak them in milk. This is especially good for breakfast dishes as it adds creaminess and a pleasant taste.

Juice Soak for Fruits: Soaking dehydrated fruits in fruit juice can enhance their sweetness and give them a more intense flavor. This works well with apples, pears, and peaches.

Safety Tip: Remember not to let the food soak for too long at room temperature, as bacteria that may have been present before drying can rehydrate and multiply. It's best to rehydrate foods in boiling water or simmering soups and stews to ensure safety.

These methods should give you a variety of options for rehydrating your dehydrated food, enhancing both the flavor and texture. Enjoy your meal preparation!

Key mistakes to steer clear of during food dehydration

While there are indeed many potential mistakes to be mindful of when dehydrating food, recognizing and avoiding these pitfalls is crucial for ensuring the safety and quality of your preserved goods. Here are some key points to keep in mind:

Not Preparing Food Properly: Before dehydrating, it's crucial to prepare your food correctly. This includes washing, peeling, and cutting your food into even sizes for consistent drying.

Overloading the Dehydrator: Placing too much food on the trays can lead to uneven drying. Make sure there's enough space for air to circulate around each piece.

Mixing Different Foods: Dehydrating different types of food at the same time can cause flavors to mix and may require different drying times, which can lead to some foods being over or under-dried.

Incorrect Temperature Settings: Each type of food has an optimal drying temperature. Using the wrong temperature can either cook the food or not dry it sufficiently.

Not Accounting for Ambient Temperature: The temperature of the room where you're dehydrating can affect the drying time. Make sure to adjust the dehydrator's settings accordingly.

Not Checking for Doneness: It's essential to check if the food is completely dried before storing it. In most cases, foods should be crispy, crunchy, or hard, and have 95% or greater of the moisture removed, unless otherwise specified in the recipe.

Buying the Wrong Dehydrator: It's important to invest in a dehydrator that suits your needs. Some may not have adequate temperature control or air circulation, which can affect the drying process.

Relying Solely on Drying Guidelines: While guidelines are helpful, they are not absolute. Factors such as your dehydrator's strength, air circulation, and the juiciness of the food can affect drying times. It's best to regularly check the progress and adjust as needed.

Dehydrating High-Fat Foods: Foods with high fat content, like butter, milk, and cheese, should be avoided as they can go rancid quickly and are difficult to dehydrate properly.

Ignoring Safety Precautions for Meat: When dehydrating meat, especially for making jerky, it's crucial to follow safety precautions to prevent bacterial growth. Use proper temperatures and acids to ensure safety.

Not Blanching Vegetables When Needed: Some vegetables require blanching before dehydrating to stop enzyme actions that can cause loss of flavor, color, and texture.

Not Rotating Trays: If your dehydrator does not have a fan to circulate the air, you should rotate the trays periodically to ensure even drying1.

Trying to Speed Up the Process: Increasing the temperature to dry food faster can be counterproductive. It's better to dehydrate at a steady, appropriate temperature.

Not Using Acidic Pretreatments When Needed: Some fruits, like apples and bananas, can brown during dehydration. Using an acidic pretreatment like lemon juice can help preserve their color.

Ignoring Humidity Levels: High humidity can extend the drying time. It's important to consider the humidity level of your environment when dehydrating food.

Improper Storage: Once dehydrated, food should be stored in airtight containers in a cool, dark place to prevent spoilage.

Not Allowing Food to Cool Before Storing: Let dehydrated food cool to room temperature before storing it to prevent condensation, which can lead to spoilage.

Not Conditioning After Dehydrating: Conditioning is the process of equalizing the moisture remaining in the dried food to prevent mold growth. After drying, store the fruit in a container, shaking it daily to distribute moisture evenly for 7 to 10 days.

Not Labeling Stored Foods: It's important to label your stored dehydrated foods with the date and contents to keep track of their shelf life and ensure proper rotation.

Using Waxed or Treated Produce: Waxed or chemically treated fruits and vegetables can prevent proper drying. Always use untreated, fresh produce for dehydration.

Not Cleaning the Dehydrator Regularly: Food particles and residues can build up over time, potentially causing flavors to transfer or bacteria to grow. Keep your dehydrator clean for safe and tasty results.

Using Sugar When Dehydrating: Adding sugar to fruits before dehydrating can create a sticky mess and does not enhance the flavor as expected. Instead, use natural sweeteners like honey or corn syrup if needed. But you can use some sugar to blanch fruits, just make sure not to place fruits covered with sugar in a dehydrator.

Dehydrating in a Poorly Ventilated Space: Good air circulation is crucial for even and effective dehydration. Make sure your dehydrating space is well-ventilate

Ignoring the Quality of Produce: Always start with high-quality produce. Dehydrating does not improve the quality of bad fruits or vegetables; it only preserves their current state.

Not Adjusting for Slice Thickness: Thicker slices take longer to dehydrate. Make sure to adjust your drying times based on the thickness of your slices.

Using Parchment Paper Incorrectly: If using parchment paper on your trays, ensure it's perforated for airflow. Non-perforated paper can block air circulation.

Dehydrating Directly After Washing: Make sure to dry your produce thoroughly after washing to avoid steaming them in the dehydrator.

Not Keeping a Dehydration Log: Keeping a log of times and temperatures for different foods can help you replicate successful batches and avoid repeating mistakes.

Using Metal Trays for Acidic Foods: Acidic foods can react with metal trays, leading to off-flavors and potential contamination. Use non-reactive trays for acidic items.

Not Following the Dehydrator's Instructions: Each dehydrator is different. Follow the manufacturer's instructions for the best results.

Ignoring Signs of Spoilage: If you notice any off-smells or discoloration in your dehydrated food, it's best to discard it to avoid the risk of foodborne illness.

By avoiding these common mistakes, you can ensure that your dehydrated foods are safe, tasty, and well-preserved. Happy dehydrating!

Foods You Should Not Dehydrate

In the following chapter, we delve into the intricacies of dehydration, highlighting specific foods that are best left out of the dehydrator. We discuss the reasons behind their unsuitability, such as high water content, fat content, and the risk of spoilage. This knowledge serves as a guide for those embarking on the journey of food preservation, ensuring the safety, quality, and success of their dehydration endeavors.

High fat content in foods like avocados, nut butter, olives, and fatty meats poses a challenge for dehydration due to several reasons. During dehydration, fats are exposed to heat and air, which can cause them to oxidize. This oxidation process leads to rancidity, where the fats break down and create off-putting flavors and smells. Consuming rancid fats is not only unpleasant but also potentially harmful, as they contain free radicals known to cause cellular and tissue damage. Moreover, the goal of dehydration is to remove water to prevent the growth of microbes. Unlike water, fat does not evaporate, so foods rich in fat may still spoil despite being dehydrated. The remaining fat can become a breeding ground for bacteria and mold, posing a risk to food safety. The texture and quality of high-fat foods are also compromised after dehydration. They often become greasy or sticky, which is not appealing. Incomplete drying of the fat can result in a product that is inconsistent and of poor quality. Lastly, one of the benefits of dehydrated foods is their extended shelf life. However, the presence of fat can drastically reduce this longevity. Over time, even at room temperature, fats can turn rancid, and the likelihood of this happening increases with higher storage temperatures. This diminishes the practicality of dehydrating high-fat foods for long-term storage, as the risk of spoilage is significantly higher. However - avocado and olives crisps are a thing, and you can try them at home. Just remember they are a snack, not a storage item.

Dairy products, such as butter, milk, cheese, and yogurt, are not good candidates for this process, as they have high moisture and fat content that can affect their safety and quality after dehydration. One of the main reasons why dairy products are not suitable for dehydration is the risk of spoilage. Dairy products contain proteins and fats that can provide a favorable environment for bacterial growth. Dehydration does not remove all the moisture from these products, leaving some water that can allow bacteria to multiply and cause spoilage. This can make the food unsafe for consumption and reduce its shelf life. Another reason why dairy products are not ideal for dehydration is the change in texture and flavor. Dehydration can alter the physical and chemical properties of dairy products, making them less appealing. For example, dehydrated milk can become lumpy and have a cooked or caramelized taste, while dehydrated cheese can become hard and brittle. These changes can affect the palatability and usability of the products. Dehydration can also affect the nutritional value of dairy products, especially the heat-sensitive vitamins and minerals. For example, dehydrated milk can lose up to 50% of its vitamin C and riboflavin content, while dehydrated cheese can lose up to 40% of its calcium and phosphorus content. These losses can reduce the health benefits of consuming dairy products. For these reasons, it's generally recommended to avoid dehydrating dairy products or to do so with caution and care.

Keep in mind: Powdered milk from the store is made with professional dehydrating machines. You should not try dehydrating milk at home, because it can spoil and grow bacteria if it stays too hot. A better way to keep milk for a long time is to freeze it or use a freeze-dryer.

While it's generally true that dairy products are not the best candidates for dehydration **cheese is a bit of an exception.** While most soft and creamy cheeses are not suitable for dehydration, some hard and semi-hard cheeses can be dehydrated successfully. These include cheddar, gouda, parmesan, feta, and romano. These cheeses have a lower moisture content, which makes them more stable and less prone to spoilage when dehydrated. However, they still require proper preparation, such as grating or slicing them thinly, and proper storage, such as using airtight containers and keeping them in a cool, dry place.

Sugar is not recommended to add while dehydrating fruits, as it can affect the texture, flavor, and shelf life of the dried fruit. Sugar can also make the fruit stickier and harder to store. If you want to sweeten your dried fruit, you can try using natural sweeteners like honey, maple syrup, or stevia. However, you should still use them sparingly and monitor the dehydration process carefully. Alternatively, you can choose fruits that are naturally sweet and ripe, and avoid adding any sweeteners at all.

Juices, soda, and liquids Dehydrating liquids like juices is impractical because the process is designed to remove water, and these items are primarily water. Canning or freezing is a better preservation method for liquids.

Eggs Dehydrating eggs is not a good idea, whether they are raw or cooked. Raw eggs can have bacteria like salmonella, which may not be killed by the low heat of the dehydrator. This can cause food poisoning and serious health problems. Cooked eggs lose their taste and texture when they are dehydrated and rehydrated. They become dry, rubbery, and unappetizing.

A better way to preserve eggs for a long time is to freeze-dry them or waterglass them. Freeze-drying removes the water from the eggs by freezing and sublimating them, which preserves their nutritional value and quality. Water-glassing involves immersing the eggs in a solution of sodium silicate, which seals the pores of the shells and prevents air and bacteria from entering. Both methods can keep eggs fresh for months or years.

Nuts are high in fat, causing them to go rancid very quickly, making them a poor choice for dehydration. However, you CAN use your dehydrator to dry out raw nuts that have been soaked.

Dehydrating is not a bad idea in general, but it requires some precautions and steps to ensure the safety and quality of the jerky. You should avoid dehydrating meats that are fatty, some type of raw, or processed. Fatty meats like bacon, sausage, ham, pork, and some beef cuts can spoil and go bad when dehydrated. Raw meats like chicken, turkey, fish, and seafood can have bacteria like salmonella or E. coli, which can make you sick if the dehydrator does not kill them. Processed meats like hot dogs, salami, pepperoni, and deli meats can have additives, preservatives, or nitrates, which can harm the jerky's quality and safety.

Fruits & veges

NOTICE! *For every food item listed below, we provide essential guidance on selection, preparation, and blanching techniques, complemented by a variety of dehydration recipes. These recipes will detail diverse cutting styles, temperature settings, and duration of dehydration to suit each product. To achieve optimal results in dehydration, it is recommended to integrate these general tips with the specific instructions provided in the recipes. This approach ensures that you harness the full benefits of the dehydration process, preserving the quality and flavor of your foods. Happy dehydrating!*

Apples

How to choose

When selecting apples for dehydration, opt for varieties that are known for their flavor and firmness. Tart apples like Granny Smith are great for a sharp flavor and hold their shape well when dehydrated. For a sweeter taste, Gala or Fuji apples are excellent choices, as they have a high sugar content that intensifies during dehydration. Look for apples that are free from blemishes and firm to the touch.

How to prepare

To prepare apples for dehydration, wash them thoroughly and slice them to the correct thickness. To minimize browning of apple slices, you can soak them in the adulated water, which is a mixture of water and an acidic substance such as vinegar or lemon juice, for about 5 to 10 minutes. For lemon juice: Mix 1 teaspoon of lemon juice with 1 cup of water. For vinegar: Combine 2 tablespoons of vinegar with 1 quart (4 cups) of water. After soaking, drain the apples well before arranging them on the dehydrator trays.

How to blanch

Blanching apples before dehydrating is not always necessary, but it can help preserve the color, texture, and flavor of the apples. If you choose to blanch, briefly boil the apple slices for 1-

2 minutes, then plunge them into ice water to stop the cooking process. Drain the apples thoroughly before dehydrating.

Apple rings: Core the apples and cut them into rings, about **1/4 inch (6 mm)** thick. Soak the apple rings in some lemon water or ascorbic acid solution for 10 minutes to prevent browning. Drain and pat dry the apple rings. Dehydrate at **130°F (54°C)** for **8 to 10 hours** or until chewy and not sticky. You should get about **1/5 pound (91 g)** of apple rings from 1 pound (454 g) of raw apples. To check for doneness, squeeze a ring between your fingers and see if it is pliable and not moist. Apple rings are a simple and tasty snack that can be eaten as they are or rehydrated in water or juice. They have a sweet and tart flavor, a light brown color, and a chewy texture.

Apple chips: Cut the apples into thin slices, about **1/8 inch (3 mm)** thick. You can use a mandolin slicer for uniform slices. Sprinkle some cinnamon or lemon juice on the slices for extra flavor. Dehydrate at **135°F (57°C)** for **6 to 8 hours**, or until crisp. You should get about **1/4 pound (113 g)** of apple chips from 1 pound (454 g) of raw apples. To check for doneness, take a slice out of the dehydrator and let it cool for a few minutes. It should be crunchy and not sticky. Apple chips are a delicious and healthy snack that can be stored in an airtight container for up to a year. They have a sweet and tangy taste, a golden brown color, and a crisp texture.

Apple cubes: Peel and core the apples and cut them into small cubes, about **1/4 inch (6 mm)** thick. Sprinkle some honey or corn syrup on the apple cubes for extra sweetness. Dehydrate at **135°F (57°C)** for **10 to 12 hours**, or until dry and firm. You should get about **1/6 pound (76 g)** of apple cubes from 1 pound (454 g) of raw apples. To check for doneness, take a cube out of the dehydrator and let it cool for a few minutes. It should be hard and not sticky. Apple cubes are a versatile and delicious snack that can be eaten as they are or added to cereals, granola bars, trail mixes, salads, or baked goods. They have a sweet and caramelized flavor, a dark brown color, and a firm texture.

Apricots

How to choose

When selecting apricots for dehydration, choose medium-sized fruits that are fully ripe but without any mold or mildew. The color should be a bright yellow to orange, as a dark color may indicate the possibility of mold inside the apricot. The fruit should be soft to the touch, indicating that the pit has detached from the body of the fruit, which is usually the perfect level of ripeness for drying. Give your fruit an extra day or two to ripen, if needed.

How to prepare

To prepare apricots for dehydration, wash the fruit thoroughly and then lay out to dry. Cut along the seam of the apricot with a sharp paring knife, splitting the apricot in half and removing the pit. Make sure to cut out any bad spots on the fruit. If you won't be consuming your dehydrated apricots within 2-3 months, consider pre-treating your fruit with lemon juice (1 cup lemon juice to 1 quart water) to prevent browning.

How to blanch

Blanching apricots before dehydrating is not typically necessary, but if you choose to do so, it can be done using a syrup blanch. Prepare a mixture of honey, light corn syrup, and water, bring it to a boil, then add the prepared fruit and simmer gently for around 10 minutes. Let them cool in the syrup for a good half hour, then lightly rinse with clean cold water before dehydrating.

Apricot chips: To make apricot chips, you need to slice fresh apricots thinly, about **1/8 inch (3 mm)** thick. You can peel the apricots or leave the skin on. Arrange the slices on a dehydrator tray in a single layer and sprinkle some honey or cinnamon on top if desired. Dehydrate at **135°F (57°C)** for **10 to 12 hours,** or until the chips are crisp and brittle. You can check for doneness by breaking a chip in half. It should snap easily and have no moisture inside. You can store the chips in an airtight container for up to a year. One pound of fresh apricots will yield about **3 ounces (85 grams)** of apricot chips. Apricot chips have a crunchy and sweet taste, a light orange color, and a thin and crisp texture. You can eat them as a snack or use them as a topping for yogurt, cereal, or ice cream.

Apricot halves: To make apricot halves, you need to cut fresh apricots in half and remove the pits. You can blanch the apricots in boiling water for a few seconds and then dip them in cold water to make the skin easier to peel off. You can also leave the skin on if you prefer. Place the apricot halves on a dehydrator tray with the cut side up and dehydrate at **135°F (57°C)** for **18 to 24 hours,** or until the halves are dry and leathery. You can check for doneness by squeezing a half with your hand. It should be firm and flexible, but not hard or brittle. You can store the halves in a ziplock bag or a glass jar for up to a year. One pound of fresh apricots will yield about **5 ounces (142 grams)** of apricot halves. Apricot halves have a chewy and fruity taste, a dark orange color, and a soft and plump texture. You can eat them as a snack or use them in salads, trail mix, granola, or baked goods.

Artichoke

How to choose

Selecting the right artichokes is the first step to successful dehydration. Look for artichokes that feel firm and heavy for their size, indicating freshness and moisture content. The leaves, or bracts, should be tightly packed and vibrant green in color, with no signs of browning at the tips. A fresh artichoke will also squeak when squeezed, confirming its crispness. Whether you choose large globe artichokes or smaller baby varieties, ensure they are free from blemishes and damage.

How to prepare

To prepare artichokes for dehydration, start by cleaning them under cold, running water. Trim the stems and remove any tough outer leaves. Cut off the top of the artichoke to expose the heart and scoop out the fuzzy choke as it's inedible. Slice the artichoke hearts into similar pieces for even drying.

How to blanch

Blanching artichokes before dehydration is recommended to enhance their safety, quality, and color retention. To blanch, immerse the artichoke pieces in boiling water for 4 minutes. Then, quickly transfer them to ice water to halt the cooking process. Drain the artichokes thoroughly and pat them dry before arranging them on the dehydrator trays.

Artichoke chips: Cut the artichoke hearts into thin slices, about **1/8 inch (0.3 cm)** thick. Blanch them in boiling water for 5 minutes to soften them and prevent browning. Drain and pat dry. Arrange the slices in a single layer on the dehydrator trays. Sprinkle some salt, pepper, garlic powder, or other seasonings of your choice. Dehydrate at **135°F (57°C)** for **6 to 8 hours**, or until crisp. You should get about **1/4 cup (15 g)** of dried artichoke chips from 1 pound (454 g) of raw artichoke hearts. Check for doneness by breaking a chip in half; it should snap easily and have no moisture inside. Artichoke chips are a delicious and healthy snack that has a nutty and slightly sweet flavor. They are crunchy and golden brown. You can enjoy them as they are or dip them in hummus, salsa, or your favorite sauce.

Artichoke powder: Cut the artichoke hearts into small pieces, about **1/4 inch (0.6 cm)** in size. Blanch them in boiling water for 5 minutes to soften them and prevent browning. Drain and pat dry. Arrange the pieces in a single layer on the dehydrator trays. Dehydrate at **135°F (57°C)** for **8 to 10 hours**, or until very dry and brittle. You should get about **2 tablespoons (6 g)** of dried artichoke pieces from 1 pound (454 g) of raw artichoke hearts. Check for doneness by crushing a piece between your fingers; it should crumble easily and have no moisture inside. Artichoke powder is a versatile and nutritious ingredient that can add flavor and fiber to your dishes. It has a mild and earthy taste that complements soups, stews, sauces, dips, dressings, and more. You can grind the dried artichoke pieces in a blender, food processor, or spice grinder to make a fine powder. Store the powder in an airtight container in a cool and dark place.

Artichoke petals: Peel off the outer leaves of the artichoke and discard the fuzzy choke. Cut the remaining leaves into halves or quarters, depending on their size. Blanch them in boiling water with some lemon juice for 10 minutes to soften them and prevent browning. Drain and pat dry. Arrange the leaves in a single layer on the dehydrator trays. Dehydrate at **125°F (52°C)** for **12 to 14 hours**, or until dry and leathery. You should get about **1 cup (40 g)** of dried artichoke petals from **1 pound (454 g)** of raw artichoke leaves. Check for doneness by tearing a leaf; it should be pliable but not moist. Artichoke petals are a flavorful and fun way to enjoy the edible part of the artichoke leaves. They have a slightly bitter and tangy taste that goes well with cheese, crackers, or bread. They are soft and green. You can rehydrate them in warm water for a few minutes to make them more tender.

Asparagus

How to choose

When selecting asparagus for dehydration, opt for young, tender stalks that are firm and upright. Look for smooth skins and unspoiled tips, and ensure the stems are not wrinkled, which can indicate dehydration or woodiness. All types of asparagus can be dehydrated, including green, white, and purple varieties, each offering a unique flavor profile. It's important to avoid any asparagus that shows signs of decay, mold, or bruising, as these defects can affect the quality of the dried product.

How to prepare

Start by washing the asparagus thoroughly to remove any dirt or debris. Cut off the tough ends of the stalks, and if desired, peel the thicker parts of the stems for even dehydration. You can then cut the asparagus into one-inch pieces or leave them whole, depending on your preference and how you plan to use them later. If you're cutting the asparagus, try to keep the pieces uniform to promote even drying.

How to blanch

Blanching asparagus before dehydrating is recommended to improve texture, speed up drying, and kill bacteria[1]. To blanch, boil the asparagus in a rolling hot water bath for 3 to 4 minutes, then quickly transfer them to ice water to stop the cooking process. This step also helps to preserve the vibrant green color and ensures a better rehydration experience later on.

Asparagus spears: Cut the asparagus into spears **4 inch (10 cm)** long and blanch them in boiling water for 2 minutes. Drain and cool them under cold water and pat them dry. Arrange the spears on the dehydrator trays and sprinkle some lemon juice and salt on top. Dehydrate at **115°F (46°C)** for **12 to 14 hours**, or until leathery. You will get about **1/5 pound (91 g)** of dried spears from 1 pound (454 g) of raw asparagus. To check for doneness, bend a spear and make sure it is dry and flexible. Asparagus spears are a simple and tasty way to preserve asparagus for later use. They have a fresh and tangy flavor and a light green color. They have a soft and chewy texture. You can rehydrate them in water or broth and use them in soups, stews, stir-fries, and more.

Asparagus flakes: Cut the asparagus into small pieces **1/4 inch (0.6 cm)** long and spread them on the dehydrator trays. Dehydrate at **125°F (52°C)** for **10 to 12 hours**, or until brittle. You will get about **1/10 pound (45 g)** of dried flakes from 1 pound (454 g) of raw asparagus. To check for doneness, crush a flake between your fingers and make sure it is dry and crumbly. Asparagus flakes are another convenient and versatile way to use dried asparagus. They have a subtle and earthy flavor and a pale green color. They have a flaky and crumbly texture. You can use them as a garnish or a seasoning for salads, pasta, rice, and more. You can also grind them into a finer powder if you prefer.

Asparagus chips: Cut the asparagus into thin slices **1/8 inch (0.3cm)** thick and spread them on the dehydrator trays. Sprinkle some salt, pepper, garlic powder, and Parmesan cheese on top. Dehydrate at **125°F (52°C)** for **6 to 8 hours**, or until crisp. You will get about **1/4 pound (113 g)** of dried chips from 1 pound (454 g) of raw asparagus. To check for doneness, break a chip in half and make sure it is dry and crunchy. Asparagus chips are a delicious and healthy snack that has a nutty and cheesy flavor. They are light green and have a crisp texture. You can enjoy them on their own or dip them in your favorite sauce.

Some tips and tricks

- Separate the tender tips, middle stalks, and tough ends, and dry them on separate trays, as they will have different drying times.

- Consider turning the tough, dried stalk ends into a powder to use as a thickener in soups and recipes.

Bananas

How to choose

Selecting the right bananas is crucial for successful dehydration. Look for bananas that are ripe, but not overly so. The skin should be yellow with just a few brown speckles, indicating they are at peak sweetness.

Bananas that are too green won't have developed their full flavor, while overripe bananas can be too mushy and may not dehydrate well. If you're planning, you can buy green bananas and monitor them as they ripen to the perfect stage for dehydration.

How to prepare

Peel the bananas and slice them uniformly to ensure even drying. The thickness of the slices can vary based on your preference, but a common recommendation is between 1/5 to 1/8 inches. To prevent browning and add a hint of citrus flavor, soak the banana slices in a mixture of lemon juice and water for about a minute. This step also acts as a preservative during the dehydration process.

How to blanch

Blanching is not a necessary step for bananas, as it is for some other fruits and vegetables. Since bananas don't benefit significantly from blanching when dehydrating, you can skip this process. The natural sugars and flavors of bananas are preserved well through dehydration without the need for blanching.

Banana chips: Cut the bananas into thin slices **1/8 inch** (**3 mm**) thick and dip them in lemon juice to prevent browning. Place them in a single layer on the dehydrator trays and dry at **135°F** (**57°C**) for **6 to 10 hours** until crisp. You will get about **1/4 pound** (**113 g**) of dried banana chips from 1 pound (**454 g**) of fresh bananas. To check for doneness, break a chip in half and look for any moisture beads. Banana chips are crunchy and sweet, with a golden yellow color. They are great for snacking, adding to granola, or making trail mix.

Banana powder: Cut the bananas into small pieces **1/4 inch** (**6 mm**) thick and dry at **135°F** (**57°C**) for **10 to 14 hours** until brittle. You will get about **1/6 pound** (**76 g**) of dried banana pieces from 1 pound (**454 g**) of fresh bananas. To check for doneness, crush a piece of banana with your fingers. It should crumble easily. Transfer the dried banana pieces to a blender or spice grinder and process until they turn into a fine powder. Banana powder is light and fluffy, with a pale yellow color. It has a mild banana flavor and can be used as a natural sweetener, a flour substitute, or a flavor enhancer. You can add banana powder to smoothies, baked goods, sauces, or desserts.

Banana coins: Cut the bananas into thick slices **1/2 inch** (**13 mm**) thick and soak them in a solution of water and ascorbic acid (vitamin C) for 10 minutes to prevent browning. Drain the bananas and place them on the dehydrator trays in a single layer. Dry at **135°F** (**57°C**) for **12 to 16 hours** until chewy and leathery. You will get about **1/5 pound** (**91 g**) of dried banana coins from 1 pound (**454 g**) of fresh bananas. To check for doneness, squeeze a coin between your fingers. It should be flexible and moist, but not sticky. Banana coins are soft and chewy, with a dark brown color. They have a sweet and tangy flavor, similar to dried apricots. They are perfect for adding to oatmeal, yogurt, or cereal.

Banana chunks: Cut the bananas into large chunks **1 inch** (**25 mm**) thick and place them in a bowl. Sprinkle some honey and cinnamon over the bananas and toss to coat. Arrange the banana chunks on the dehydrator trays in a single layer and dry at **135°F** (**57°C**) for **18 to 22 hours** until firm and dry. You will get about **1/7 pound** (**65 g**) of dried banana chunks from 1 pound (**454 g**) of fresh bananas. To check for doneness, bite into a chunk and look for any moisture. Banana chunks are hard and dense, with a deep brown color. They have a caramelized and spicy flavor, reminiscent of banana bread. They are ideal for making energy bars, cookies, or muffins.

Beets

How to choose

- Select fresh beets that are firm to the touch with smooth skins and deep, vibrant colors. Smaller beets tend to be sweeter and more tender, making them ideal for dehydration.
- The beets should have their greens intact, which indicates freshness. However, remove the greens before dehydrating and use them in other dishes if desired.

- Avoid beets that have soft spots, bruises, or shriveled skins, as these can affect the quality and taste of the dehydrated product.

How to prepare

- Wash the beets thoroughly under cold running water to remove any dirt or debris. Use a vegetable brush if necessary to ensure they are clean.
- Trim off the beet tops and roots, and peel the beets with a vegetable peeler to remove the outer skin, which can be tough.
- Slice the beets into uniform, thin slices. A mandolin slicer can help achieve consistent thickness.

How to blanch

- To blanch, bring a large pot of water to a rolling boil. Add the beet slices and blanch for 3 to 5 minutes, depending on their thickness.
- After blanching, immediately transfer the beets to a bowl of ice water to halt the cooking process. This will help maintain their vibrant color.
- Drain the beets well and pat them dry with a clean kitchen towel or paper towel to remove excess moisture.

Beet cubes: Cut the beets into small cubes, about **1/4 inch (6.4 mm)** thick. You can peel the beets or leave the skin on, depending on your preference. Blanch the cubes in boiling water for about 5 minutes to soften them and preserve their color. Drain the cubes and pat them dry with a paper towel. Spread the cubes evenly on the dehydrator trays and dehydrate at **125°F (52°C)** for **12 to 14 hours** or until dry and hard. You should get about **1/3 cup (40 g)** of beet cubes from 1 pound (454 g) of raw beets. Check for doneness by biting a cube; it should be crunchy and not moist. Beet cubes are hard, dense, and slightly sweet, with a dark red color. You can use them to make soups, stews, salads, or snacks. You can also rehydrate them by soaking them in water for about an hour before using them.

Beet jerky: Cut the beets into thin strips, about **1/8 inch (3.2 mm)** thick. You can marinate the strips in a mixture of soy sauce, honey, garlic, ginger, and spices for extra flavor, or just season them with salt and pepper. Arrange the strips on the dehydrator trays and dehydrate them at **145°F (63°C)** for **4 to 6 hours,** or until chewy and dry. You should get about **1/2 cup (60 g)** of beet jerky from 1 pound (454 g) of raw beets. Check for doneness by bending a strip; it should be flexible and not break. Beet jerky is chewy, savory, and slightly sweet, with a dark red color. It makes a satisfying and protein-rich snack or a vegan alternative to meat jerky.

Beet chips: Cut the beets into thin slices, about **1/16 inch (1.6 mm)** thick. You can use a mandolin slicer for uniform slices. Place the slices in a single layer on the dehydrator trays and sprinkle some salt or your favorite seasoning on top. Dehydrate at **135°F (57°C)** for **6 to 8 hours**, or until crisp. You should get about **1/4 cup (15 g)** of beet chips from 1 pound (454 g) of raw beets. Check for doneness by breaking a chip in half; it should snap easily and not bend. Beet chips are crunchy, sweet, and earthy, with a deep red color. They make a great snack or a healthy alternative to potato chips.

Beet powder: Cut the beets into small pieces, about **1/4 inch (6.4 mm)** thick. You can peel the beets or leave the skin on, depending on your preference. Spread the pieces evenly on the dehydrator trays and dehydrate at **125°F (52°C)** for **10 to 12 hours**, or until dry and brittle. You should get about **1/3 cup (30 g)** of beet pieces from 1 pound (454 g) of raw beets. Check for doneness by crushing a piece between your fingers; it should crumble easily and not stick. Beet powder is fine, smooth, and intensely flavored, with a vibrant red color. You can use it to add color and flavor to smoothies, soups, sauces, baked goods, and more.

Bell peppers

How to Choose

The key to dehydrating bell peppers starts with choosing the right ones. Opt for firm, bright, and wrinkle-free peppers. They should feel heavy for their size, indicating they are full of moisture and ripe. The skin should be taut and glossy without any soft spots, blemishes, or signs of decay. While any color bell pepper can be dehydrated, red, yellow, and orange varieties tend to be sweeter and more flavorful than green.

How to Prepare

To prepare bell peppers for dehydration, start by washing them under cold running water. Slice off the top and bottom. Remove the core and seeds, and slice the peppers into uniform strips or rings. This ensures that they will dry evenly. Lay the pepper pieces out on the dehydrator trays, making sure they don't overlap, as this could result in uneven drying.

How to Blanch

To blanch, boil water in a large pot and submerge the pepper slices for about three minutes. Then, quickly move them to an ice water bath to stop the cooking process. Drain the peppers well and pat them dry before placing them on the dehydrator trays.

Bell pepper cubes: Cut the bell peppers into small cubes, about **1/4 inch (0.6 cm)** on each side. Spread them on the dehydrator trays and dry at **125°F (52°C)** for **8 to 10 hours**. You should get about **1/3 cup (20 g)** of dried cubes from **1 pound (454 g)** of raw bell peppers. Check for doneness by squeezing a piece; it should be hard and not spongy. Bell pepper cubes have a firm texture and a rich and sweet flavor. They are ideal for adding some crunch and sweetness to rice, pasta, couscous, or quinoa dishes. You can also rehydrate them and use them in stir-fries, omelets, or frittatas.

Bell pepper strips: Cut the bell peppers into long strips, about **1/4 inch (0.6 cm)** wide and **2 inch (5 cm)** long. Lay them on the dehydrator trays and dry them at **135°F (57°C)** for **10 to 12 hours**. You should get about **1/2 cup (30 g)** of dried strips from **1 pound (454 g)** of raw bell peppers. Check for doneness by twisting a piece; it should be flexible and not moist. Bell pepper strips have a soft texture and a fruity and sweet flavor. They are wonderful for adding some color and flavor to salads, sandwiches, burgers, or wraps. You can also rehydrate them and use them in dips, salsas, or relishes.

Bell pepper flakes: Cut the bell peppers into thin slices, about **1/8 inch (0.3 cm)** thick. Spread them evenly on the dehydrator trays and dry at **135°F (57°C)** for **8 to 10 hours**. You should get about **1/4 cup (15 g)** of dried flakes from **1 pound (454 g)** of raw bell peppers. Check for doneness by breaking a piece in half; it should be brittle and snap easily. Bell pepper flakes have a bright color and a sweet and tangy flavor. They are great for adding some spice and color to soups, stews, sauces, pizzas, and salads. You can also grind them into a fine powder and use it as a seasoning.

Bell pepper chips: Cut the bell peppers into rings, about **1/4 inch (0.6 cm)** thick. Remove the seeds and membranes. Arrange them on the dehydrator trays and dry at **125°F (52°C)** for **6 to 8 hours**. You should get about **1/2 cup (30 g)** of dried chips from **1 pound (454 g)** of raw bell peppers. Check for doneness by bending a piece; it should be crisp and not pliable. Bell pepper chips have a crunchy texture and a mild and sweet flavor. They are perfect for snacking on their own or dipping into hummus, salsa, or guacamole. You can also rehydrate them and use them in salads, sandwiches, or wraps.

Blackberries

How to Choose

Selecting the right blackberries is crucial for a successful dehydration process. Look for ripe, plump, and firm berries that are uniform. They should be deep purple to black, without any signs of mold or bruising. Organic or wild blackberries are preferable as they are free from pesticides and chemicals. If you're picking your own, choose berries that come off the stem with a gentle tug a sign they're perfectly ripe.

How to Prepare

Before dehydrating, thoroughly wash the blackberries in cold water to remove any dirt or insects. Gently pat them dry with a clean towel or use a salad spinner to remove excess moisture. If the berries are particularly large, you may slice them in half to ensure even drying. Arrange the blackberries on dehydrator trays in a single layer, ensuring they do not touch or overlap, which could lead to uneven drying.

How to Blanch

Blanching is not typically required for blackberries due to their thin skins and small size. However, if you wish to soften the skins and potentially reduce the dehydration time, you can blanch the berries by briefly immersing them in boiling water for 30 seconds to 1 minute. Immediately transfer the blanched blackberries to an ice bath to halt the cooking process. Drain and proceed with the dehydration steps as outlined above.

Whole blackberries: To dehydrate whole blackberries, you need to wash and drain them well. You can leave the stems on or remove them according to your preference. Place the whole blackberries on a dehydrator tray in a single layer, leaving some space between them. Set the temperature to **115°F (46°C)** and dry for **24 to 36 hours**. You should get about **1/2 cup (60 g)** of dried whole blackberries from 1 pound (454 g) of raw. To check for doneness, the blackberries should be dry and wrinkled, but still soft and plump. You can then store them in an airtight container or a ziplock bag. Whole blackberries have a **dark purple color** and a **juicy and sweet flavor**. They can be eaten as a **snack** or a **trail mix** ingredient, or rehydrated and used in **baking**, **cooking**, or **making jams**.

Blackberry powder: To make blackberry powder, you need to slice the blackberries into 1/4 inch (0.6 cm) pieces and spread them on a dehydrator tray. Set the temperature to **135°F (57°C)** and dry for **8 to 10 hours**. You should get about **1/4 cup (30 g)** of dried blackberries from 1 pound (454 g) of raw. To check for doneness, the blackberries should be crisp and brittle. You can then grind them into a fine powder using a blender or a spice grinder. Blackberry powder has a **deep purple color** and a **sweet and tangy flavor**. It can be used to **add color and flavor** to smoothies, yogurt, oatmeal, baked goods, and more.

Blackberry chips: To make blackberry chips, you need to cut the blackberries in half and place them cut-side up on a dehydrator tray. Set the temperature to **125°F (52°C)** and dry for **12 to 14 hours**. You should get about **1/3 cup (40 g)** of blackberry chips from 1 pound (454 g) of raw. To check for doneness, the blackberries should be crunchy and not moist. Blackberry chips have a **bright red color** and a **crispy and tart flavor**. They can be eaten as a **crunchy snack** or a **garnish** for salads, ice cream, or cakes.

Blueberries

How to choose

The best blueberries for dehydration are fresh, ripe, and juicy. They should have a smooth skin and a firm flesh. Avoid blueberries that are green, wrinkled, bruised, or have soft spots.

You can use any variety of blueberries, such as wild, cultivated, or hybrid, depending on your preference and availability. Each variety has a slightly different flavor, sweetness, and size. Wild blueberries are smaller and tarter than cultivated blueberries, which are larger and sweeter. Hybrid blueberries are a cross between wild and cultivated blueberries and have a balanced flavor and size.

How to prepare

• Wash the blueberries thoroughly under running water, and remove any dirt or insects. You can also soak them in a solution of water and vinegar for 15 minutes to disinfect them and remove any residue.

• Pierce the skin of each blueberry with a knife, a fork, or a toothpick. This will help the moisture escape and prevent the blueberries from bursting during dehydration. You can also blanch the blueberries in boiling water for 30 seconds, and then plunge them into ice water to stop the cooking process. This will also crack the skin and preserve the color of the blueberries.

• Dry the blueberries well in a salad spinner or by gently patting them with a clean towel. Excess moisture can prevent the blueberries from drying evenly and quickly.

How to blanch

• Blanching is an optional step that can help preserve the color, flavor, and nutrients of the blueberries. It involves briefly boiling the blueberries in water or corn syrup, and then plunging them into ice water to stop the cooking process.

• To blanch the blueberries in water, bring a large pot of water to a boil, and add a pinch of salt and a splash of lemon juice. This can help keep the blueberries bright and fresh. Add the blueberries in batches, and boil them for about 30 seconds. Then, transfer them to a bowl of ice water, and drain them well.

• To blanch the blueberries in corn syrup, combine 4 cups of water and 2 cups of sugar in a large pot, and bring it to a boil. Stir until the dissolves, and add a splash of lemon juice. This can help enhance the flavor and sweetness of the blueberries. Add the blueberries in batches, and simmer them for about 5 minutes. Then, transfer them to a bowl of ice water, and drain them well.

• Blanching can help prevent the blueberries from browning or losing their flavor during dehydration. However, it can also make them softer and stickier, and add extra sugar to the final product. You can skip this step if you prefer.

Blueberry candy: Coat whole blueberries with some honey, maple syrup, or agave nectar and place them on the dehydrator trays. Set the temperature to **145°F (63°C)** and dry for **18 to 20 hours**, or until the blueberries are shriveled and sticky. Check for doneness by squeezing a berry and tasting it. It should be chewy and sweet, but not mushy or sour. Blueberry candy is soft and sticky, with a dark purple color and a rich and sweet flavor. It can be eaten as a candy, mixed with nuts or seeds, or used as a filling for pastries or chocolates.

Blueberry chips: Cut the blueberries in half about **0.25 inch (0.6cm)** thick and place them on the dehydrator trays with the cut side up. Set the temperature to **135°F (57°C)** and dry for **8 to 10 hours**, or until crisp and brittle. Check for doneness by breaking a chip in half and looking for any moisture beads. Blueberry chips are crunchy and sweet, with a dark purple color and a concentrated berry flavor. They are great for snacking, adding to granola, or topping yogurt or ice cream.

Blueberry powder: Cut the blueberries in quarters about **1/8 inch (0.3cm)** thick and place them on the dehydrator trays in a single layer. Set the temperature to **125°F (52°C)** and dry for **12 to 14 hours**, or until very dry and hard. Check for doneness by crushing a piece between your fingers and feeling for any stickiness. Blueberry powder is fine and powdery, with a deep blue color and a tart and sweet flavor. It can be used to make smoothies, sauces, jams, baked goods, or cosmetics.

Broccoli

How to choose

The best broccoli for dehydration is fresh, crisp, and green. They should have a tight and firm head with no yellow or brown spots. Avoid broccoli that are limp, wilted, or have holes or insects.

You can use any variety of broccoli, such as calabrese, romanesco, or purple sprouting, depending on your preference and availability.

How to prepare

Wash the broccoli thoroughly under running water, and remove any dirt or insects. You can also soak them in a solution of water and vinegar for 15 minutes to sanitize them and remove any residue.

Cut or break the broccoli using a knife or your hands. You can also use a food processor to chop the broccoli into smaller pieces if you want to make broccoli powder.

How to blanch

To blanch the broccoli in water, bring a large pot of water to a boil, and add a pinch of baking soda. This can help keep the broccoli green and bright. Add the broccoli pieces in batches, and boil them for about 1 minute. Then, transfer them to a bowl of ice water, and drain them well.

Dry the broccoli well by gently patting them with a clean towel. Excess moisture can prevent the broccoli from drying evenly and quickly.

Blanching can help prevent the broccoli from browning or losing its flavor during dehydration. However, it can also make them softer and less crispy, and add extra salt or sodium to the final product. You can skip this step if you prefer, or experiment with different blanching times and methods to find your preferred result.

Broccoli chips: Cut the broccoli into thin slices about **1/8 inch (0.3 cm)** thick and arrange them in a single layer on the dehydrator trays. Sprinkle some salt, pepper, garlic powder, or other seasonings of your choice over the slices. Dehydrate at **125°F (52°C)** for **6 to 8 hours**, or until crisp and brittle. You should get about **1/4 cup (15 g)** of dried broccoli chips from 1 pound (454 g) of raw broccoli. To check for doneness, break a chip in half and see if it snaps easily. If it bends or feels moist, it needs more drying time. Broccoli chips are a delicious and healthy snack that can be eaten on their own or dipped in your favorite sauce. They have a crunchy texture and a slightly nutty flavor. You can store them in an airtight container for up to a year.

Broccoli jerky: Cut the broccoli into thick strips about **1/4 inch (0.6 cm)** thick and marinate them in a mixture of soy sauce, honey, vinegar, garlic, ginger, and red pepper flakes for at least 2 hours, or overnight in the refrigerator. Drain the excess marinade and arrange the strips on the dehydrator trays. Dehydrate at **135°F (57°C)** for **4 to 6 hours**, or until chewy and leathery. You should get about **1/2 cup (30 g)** of dried broccoli jerky from 1 pound (454 g) of raw broccoli. To check for doneness, bend a strip and see if it tears easily. If it breaks or crumbles, it is over-dried. Broccoli jerky is a savory and spicy snack that can be enjoyed as a protein-rich alternative to meat jerky. It has a chewy texture and a complex flavor. You can store it in an airtight container for up to a month.

Broccoli granola: Cut the broccoli into small florets about **1/2 inch (1.3cm)** in diameter and blanch them as described above. Toss them with some oats, nuts, seeds, dried fruits, honey, oil, cinnamon, and salt in a large bowl. Spread the mixture on the dehydrator trays and dehydrate at **145°F (63°C)** for **10 to 12 hours**, or until crisp and golden. To check for doneness, taste a piece and see if it is crunchy and sweet. If it is chewy or bitter, it needs more drying time. Broccoli granola is a nutritious and delicious breakfast or snack that can be eaten with milk, yogurt, or by itself. It has a crunchy texture and a sweet and spicy flavor. You can store it in an airtight container for up to a month.

Brussels sprouts

How to choose

Selecting the right Brussels sprouts is essential for a successful dehydration process. Look for sprouts that are firm and heavy for their size, which indicates freshness and moisture content. The leaves should be tightly packed and vibrant green, with no signs of browning at the tips. If you find Brussels sprouts on the stalk, opt for those, as they tend to stay fresher for a longer period.

How to prepare

To prepare Brussels sprouts for dehydration, start by rinsing them under cold water. If necessary, peel off the small outer leaves and trim the hard-stem base to make it easier to cut the sprouts in half. This will also give you a flat bottom for safer slicing.

How to blanch

Blanching Brussels sprouts before dehydrating are recommended to enhance their quality and safety. Blanching improves color and texture, relaxes tissues so pieces dry faster, and helps destroy potentially harmful bacteria. To blanch, boil the sprouts for 3-5 minutes, then drain and immediately transfer them to an ice bath to cool. Pat it dry or pat dry with paper towels before dehydrating.

Brussels Sprouts Leaves: Peel off the outer leaves of the Brussels sprouts and discard any that are damaged or yellow. Carefully separate individual leaves. You can leave them whole or cut them into smaller pieces **1/2 inch (1.3 cm)** if you prefer. Spread them on the dehydrator trays in a single layer and dry at **125°F (52°C)** for **4 to 6 hours**, or until crisp and crumbly. You should get about **2 cups (473 ml)** of dried leaves from 1 pound (0.45 kg) of raw Brussels sprouts. Check for doneness by crushing a leaf in your hand and seeing if it turns into powder. Brussels sprouts leaves are crunchy, slightly bitter, and have a bright green color. You can use them to make tea, seasonings, garnishes, or salads.

Brussels Sprout Halves: Cut the Brussels sprouts in half and steam them for **5 minutes**. Let them cool slightly and squeeze out the excess water. Spread them on the dehydrator trays and dry at **145°F (63°C)** for **8 to 10 hours,** or until leathery and pliable. You should get about **2 cups** (473 ml) of dried halves from **1 pound (0.45 kg)** of raw Brussels sprouts. Check for doneness by bending it a half and seeing if it is flexible and not brittle. Brussels sprout halves are chewy, sweet, and have a nutty flavor. You can use them to make soups, stews, curries, and gratins.

Brussels Sprout Chips: Cut the Brussels sprouts into thin slices (**1/8 inch** or **0.3 cm**) and toss them with some oil, salt, and your favorite seasonings. Spread them in a single layer on the dehydrator trays and dry at **135°F (57°C)** for **6 to 8 hours,** or until crisp. You should get about **1/4 cup (59 ml)** of dried chips from **1 pound (0.45 kg)** of raw Brussels sprouts. Check for doneness by breaking a chip in half and seeing if it snaps easily. Brussels sprout chips are crunchy, salty, and slightly bitter, with a dark green color. They are great for snacking or adding to salads and soups.

Butternut squash

How to choose

Choose fresh, ripe, and firm butternut squash with smooth and tan skin and a heavyweight. The squash should have no signs of cracks, bruises, or mold. You can use any variety of butternut squash, such as Waltham, Butterbush, or Metro, depending on your preference and availability.

Avoid using unripe, overripe, or damaged butternut squash, as they will not dehydrate well and may affect the taste and texture of the final product.

How to prepare

• Wash the butternut squash under cold running water and dry it with a paper towel or a clean cloth.

• Cut off the stem and the bottom of the butternut squash and discard them. Cut the squash in half and scoop out the seeds and the fibers with a spoon. You can also roast the seeds for a snack or use them for planting.

• Peel the skin off the butternut squash with a knife or a vegetable peeler. Cut the flesh using a sharp knife or a food processor. Try to make the cubes or slices as uniform as possible for even drying.

How to blanch

• Blanching is recommended for dehydrating butternut squash, as it will help retain the natural color and prevent the cubes from becoming hard and woody.

• To blanch butternut squash, bring a large pot of water to a boil. Add the butternut squash cubes and boil for about 3 minutes, then drain and rinse them under cold water to stop the cooking process.

• Alternatively, you can steam the butternut squash for about 5 minutes over boiling water, then cool them under cold water.

• After blanching, pat them dry with a paper towel or a clean cloth before placing them on dehydrator trays.

Butternut squash chips: Cut the butternut squash into thin slices, about **1/8 inch (3 mm)** thick. You can peel the squash or leave the skin on for extra crunch. Season the slices with salt, pepper, and any spices you like, such as paprika, garlic powder, or cinnamon. Arrange the slices in a single layer on the dehydrator trays and dry at **135°F (57°C)** for **6 to 8 hours**, or until crisp. You should get about **1/4 cup (15 g)** of dried chips from 1 pound (454 g) of raw squash. To check for doneness, break a chip in half and look for any moisture beads. The chips should be dry and crunchy, with a golden-orange color and a sweet and savory flavor. You can enjoy them as a snack, or use them to make nachos, salads, or dips.

Butternut squash leather: Peel and chop the butternut squash into large pieces. Boil them in water until soft, then drain and mash them. You can add some honey, maple syrup to sweeten the mash, and some lemon juice, vanilla extract, or pumpkin spice to enhance the flavor. Spread the mash evenly on a parchment paper-lined dehydrator tray, about **1/4 inch (6 mm)** thick. Dry at **140°F (60°C)** for **6 to 8 hours**, or until pliable. You should get about **1/2 cup (75 g)** of dried leather from 1 pound (454 g) of raw squash. To check for doneness, peel off a piece of leather and see if it is sticky or moist. The leather should be dry and chewy, with a dark orange color and a sweet and spicy flavor. You can cut it into strips or shapes, and roll it up for easy storage. You can eat it as a snack, or use it to make candy, granola bars, or trail mix.

Butternut squash jerky: Cut the butternut squash into thin strips, about **1/4 inch (6 mm)** thick and **3 inch (7.6 cm)** long. You can peel the squash or leave the skin on for extra texture.

After preparing, arrange them on the dehydrator trays and dry them at **155°F (68°C)** for **8 to 10 hours**, or until chewy. You should get about **1/3 cup (50 g)** of dried jerky from **1 pound (454 g)** of raw squash. To check for doneness, bend a strip and see if it cracks but does not break.

Cabbage

How to choose

- Choose fresh, firm, and green cabbage with no signs of wilting, browning, or insect damage. The head should be compact, and the leaves should be crisp. You can use any variety of cabbage, such as green, red, or savoy, depending on your preference and availability.
- Avoid using old, soft, or rotten cabbage, as they will not dehydrate well and may affect the taste and texture of the final product.

How to prepare

- Wash the cabbage under cold running water and drain it well. Pat it dry with a paper towel or a clean cloth.
- Cut off the core and the outer leaves of the cabbage and discard them. Cut the head into quarters and then into thin strips, using a sharp knife or a mandolin slicer. Try to make the strips as uniform as possible for even drying.
- Spread the cabbage strips in a single layer on dehydrator trays, leaving some space between them for air circulation. Do not overcrowd the trays, preparing them, or the cabbage will take longer to dry.

How to blanch

- Blanching is recommended for dehydrating cabbage, as it will help retain the natural color and prevent the strips from becoming tough and rubbery.
- To blanch cabbage, bring a large pot of water to a boil and add some salt. Add the cabbage strips and boil for about 2 minutes, then drain and rinse them under cold water to stop the cooking process.
- Alternatively, you can steam the cabbage strips for about 4 minutes over boiling water, then cool them under cold water.
- After blanching, pat the cabbage strips dry with a paper towel or a clean cloth before placing them on dehydrator trays.

Cabbage chips: Cut the cabbage into thin slices, about **1/8 inch (3 mm)** thick. After preparing, spread them on the dehydrator trays in a single layer. Sprinkle some salt, pepper, and your favorite seasoning on top. Dehydrate at **125°F (52°C)** for **6 to 8 hours**, or until crisp. You can get about **1/4 cup (15 g)** of dried cabbage chips from 1 pound (454 g) of raw cabbage. To check for doneness, break a chip in half and make sure it is dry and crunchy. Cabbage chips are a delicious and healthy snack that you can enjoy anytime. They have a light and crispy texture and a mild and slightly sweet flavor. You can store them in an airtight container for up to a year.

Cabbage powder: Cut the cabbage into small pieces, about **1/4 inch (6 mm)** or smaller. After preparing, spread them on the dehydrator trays in a single layer. Dehydrate at **135°F (57°C)** for **8 to 10 hours**, or until brittle. You can get about **1/3 cup (20 g)** of dried cabbage pieces from 1 pound (454 g) of raw cabbage. To check for doneness, crush a piece between your fingers and make sure it is dry and powdery. Cabbage powder is a versatile and nutritious ingredient that you can use to add flavor and color to soups, stews, sauces, dips, smoothies, and more. It has a concentrated and slightly bitter taste, and a fine and smooth texture.

Cantaloupe

How to choose

The quality of the Cantaloupe you start with will affect the taste and texture of the dehydrated product. You want to choose a ripe and flavorful Cantaloupe that feels heavy for its size and has a good color. Avoid Cantaloupes that are bruised, cracked, or have soft spots. You can also tap the Cantaloupe and listen for a hollow sound, which indicates ripeness. The Cantaloupe should also have a sweet and fruity aroma at the stem end.

How to prepare

To prepare the cantaloupe for dehydration, you need to wash it well and cut it in half. Scoop out the seeds and the stringy parts from the center and discard them. Then, place the flat side of the Cantaloupe on a cutting board and slice it into thin sections, about 1/4 to 1/2 inch thick, depending on your preferences, you can find some ideas in the recipes below. Remove the skin from the slices and cut them into smaller pieces, about 2 inch wide. You can also use a Cantaloupe baller or a cookie cutter to make different shapes.

How to blanch

Blanching is not necessary for dehydrating cantaloupe, as it does not affect the color, flavor, or texture of the fruit. However, some people prefer to blanch cantaloupe to reduce the drying time and to kill any bacteria or enzymes that may cause spoilage. To blanch melon, you need to bring a large pot of water to a boil and add some lemon juice or citric acid to prevent browning. Then, add the melon pieces in small batches and boil them for about 30 seconds. Drain the cantaloupe and plunge it into ice water to stop the cooking process. Pat them dry with paper towels before dehydrating them.

Cantaloupe slices: Cut the Cantaloupe into thin slices, about **1/4 inch (6 mm)** thick. After preparing, spread the slices on the dehydrator trays in a single layer. Set the temperature to **135°F (57°C)** and dry for **8 to 10 hours**. Check for doneness by bending a slice, it should be flexible and not sticky. Cantaloupe slices are chewy and sweet, with a refreshing Cantaloupe flavor and aroma. They have a light orange or green color and a flat shape. You can enjoy them as a snack, use them as a topping for yogurt, cereal, or ice cream, or rehydrate them and use them as a filling for pies, cakes, or pastries.

Cantaloupe candy: Cut the Cantaloupe into small pieces, about **1/4 inch (6 mm)** in size. Remove any seeds and rind, transfer the pieces to a large pot, and add enough water to cover them. Bring to a boil and then reduce the heat and simmer for 20 to 30 minutes, stirring occasionally, until the Cantaloupe is soft and mushy. Mash the Cantaloupe with a potato masher or a fork, and add 2 cups (400 g) of honey and 1/4 cup (60 ml) of lemon juice. Cook over medium-high heat, stirring constantly, until the mixture is thick and sticky.

Drop the mixture by teaspoonfuls onto a baking mat lined with parchment paper and let it cool completely. Place it on the dehydrator trays in a single layer. Set the temperature to **135°F (57°C)** and dry for **8 to 10 hours**, or until the candy is dry and chewy. Check for doneness by biting into a candy; it should be soft and sticky, but not wet. Cantaloupe candies are chewy and sweet, with a tangy Cantaloupe flavor and aroma. You can enjoy them as a treat, or use them as a decoration for cakes or cupcakes.

Cantaloupe chips: Cut the Cantaloupe into thick slices, about **1/8 inch (3 mm)** thick. After preparing, sprinkle some honey, cinnamon, and nutmeg over the slices and toss to coat. Spread the slices on the dehydrator trays in a single layer. Set the temperature to **145°F (63°C)** and dry for **10 to 12 hours**, or until the slices are crisp and crunchy. Check for doneness by biting into a slice; it should not be chewy or moist. Cantaloupe chips are crispy and sweet, with a spicy Cantaloupe flavor and aroma. You can enjoy them as a snack, or serve them with whipped cream, custard, or chocolate sauce.

#

How to choose

Choose fresh and firm carrots that have no signs of wilting, cracking, or rotting. Fresh carrots will have a bright orange color and smooth skin. You can use any variety of carrots, such as baby carrots, large carrots, or rainbow carrots.

How to prepare

- Wash the carrots thoroughly and peel them if desired. Washing the carrots will remove any dirt, insects, or pesticides that may be on the surface. Peeling the carrots will remove the outer layer of skin, which may have a bitter taste or a tough texture.

- Trim the ends and cut the carrots, depending on your preference. Thin slices or shreds will dehydrate faster and more evenly than thick or whole carrots.

How to blanch

- Blanching is necessary for dehydrating carrots, as it will prevent them from turning brown and losing their flavor and nutrients. However, blanching can also cause some nutrient loss and flavor change, so it should be done in the shortest time possible.

- To blanch your carrots, you will need a large pot of water, a large bowl of ice water, a slotted spoon, and a colander.

- Bring a large pot of water to a boil and add a pinch of salt. Salt will help the carrots retain their color and flavor.

- Add the carrot slices or shreds to the boiling water and cook for 3 to 5 minutes, depending on the size and thickness of the pieces. Do not overcook the carrots, as they will become mushy and lose their texture and nutrients.

- Use a slotted spoon to transfer the carrots from the boiling water to the ice water. The ice water will stop the cooking process and cool the carrots quickly.

- Drain the carrots well in a colander and pat them dry with a clean towel or paper towel.

Carrot coins: Cut the carrots into thin rounds about **1/8 inch (3 mm)** thick. Dehydrate at **125°F (52°C)** for **8 to 10 hours** until crisp and brittle. You can get about **1/4 cup (60 ml)** of dried carrot coins from 1 pound (454 g) of raw carrots. To check for doneness, break a coin in half and look for any moist spots in the center. If there are none, the coins are done. Carrot coins have a bright orange color, a sweet and earthy flavor, and a crunchy texture. They are great for snacking, adding to soups and stews, or making carrot chips with seasonings.

Carrot shreds: Shred the carrots coarsely with a box grater or a food processor with a shredding blade. Dehydrate at **135°F (57°C)** for **6 to 8 hours** until leathery and tough. You can get about **1/3 cup (80 ml)** of dried carrot shreds from 1 pound (454 g) of raw carrots. To check for doneness, squeeze a handful of shreds and see if they spring back or stick together. If they spring back, they are done. A tip for shredding the carrots quickly is to cut them into smaller pieces before grating. Carrot shreds have a vibrant orange color, a mild and sweet flavor, and a chewy texture. They are perfect for adding to salads, sandwiches, wraps, or making carrot cake.

Carrot chips: Cut the carrots into thin slices about **1/8 inch (3 mm)** thick. Coat them with a mixture of oil, salt, and your favorite seasonings. Dehydrate at **145°F (63°C)** for **4 to 6 hours** until crisp and golden. You can get about **2 cups (480 ml)** of dried carrot chips from 1 pound (454 g) of raw carrots. To check for doneness, taste a chip and see if it is crunchy and flavorful. If it is, it is done. A tip for making the carrot chips is to use a baking sheet lined with parchment paper to prevent sticking. Carrot chips have a dark orange color, a spicy and salty flavor, and a crispy texture. They are delicious for snacking, topping salads, or serving with dips.

Cauliflower

How to choose

- Choose fresh, firm, and white cauliflower with no signs of browning, wilting, or insect damage. The florets should be tight, and the leaves should be green. You can use any variety of cauliflower, such as white, purple, orange, or green, depending on your preference and availability.

- Avoid using old, soft, or yellow cauliflower, as they will not dehydrate well and may affect the taste and texture of the final product.

How to prepare

- Wash the cauliflower under cold running water and drain it well. Pat it dry with a paper towel or a clean cloth.

- Cut off the stem and the leaves of the cauliflower and discard them. Cut the head into small florets, using a sharp knife or kitchen scissors. You can also use a food processor or a blender to chop the florets but be careful not to overprocess them, or they will turn into crumbs.

- Spread the cauliflower florets in a single layer on dehydrator trays, leaving some space between them for air circulation. Do not overcrowd the trays, or the cauliflower will take longer to dry.

How to blanch

- Blanching is recommended for dehydrating cauliflower, as it will help retain the natural color and prevent the florets from becoming hard and brittle.

- To blanch cauliflower, bring a large pot of water to a boil and add some salt. Add the cauliflower florets and boil for about 3 minutes, then drain and rinse them under cold water to stop the cooking process.

- Alternatively, you can steam the cauliflower florets for about 5 minutes over boiling water, then cool them under cold water.

- After blanching, pat the cauliflower florets dry with a paper towel or a clean cloth before placing them on dehydrator trays.

Cauliflower rice: Cut the cauliflower into small florets and pulse them in a food processor until they resemble rice grains. Spread them on a dehydrator tray in a thin layer and dehydrate at **125°F (52°C)** for **4 to 6 hours**. You will get about **1/4 pound (113 g)** of dried cauliflower rice from 1 pound (454 g) of raw cauliflower. To check for doneness, squeeze a handful of the rice and see if it crumbles easily. Cauliflower rice is a low-carb and gluten-free alternative to regular rice. It has a mild and nutty flavor and a fluffy texture. You can use it to make pilaf, risotto, or any other dish that calls for rice.

Cauliflower popcorn: Cut the cauliflower into small florets, about **1/2 inch (1.3 cm)** in diameter. Toss them with some oil, salt, nutritional yeast, and paprika. Spread them on a dehydrator tray in a single layer and dehydrate at **145°F (63°C)** for **8 to 10 hours**. You will get about **1/5 pound (91 g)** of dried cauliflower popcorn from 1 pound (454 g) of raw cauliflower. To check for doneness, bite a piece and see if it is crunchy and dry. Cauliflower popcorn is a vegan and low-calorie version of popcorn. It has a cheesy and smoky flavor and a crunchy texture. You can eat it as a snack or sprinkle it on salads, soups, or casseroles for some extra crunch.

Cauliflower slices: Cut the cauliflower into thick slices, about **1/4 inch (6 mm)** thick. After preparing, arrange the slices on a dehydrator tray in a single layer and dehydrate at **155°F (68°C)** for **10 to 12 hours**. You will get about **1/10 pound (45 g)** of dried cauliflower jerky from 1 pound (454 g) of raw cauliflower. To check for doneness, bend a slice and see if it is chewy and leathery. Cauliflower jerky is a meatless and high-protein snack that can satisfy your cravings. It has a sweet flavor and a chewy texture. You can eat it as it is or cut it into smaller pieces and add it to salads, sandwiches, or wraps.

Celery

How to choose

- Choose fresh, crisp, and green celery with no signs of wilting, browning, or insect damage. The stalks should be firm, and the leaves should be bright. You can use any variety of celery, such as Pascal, Utah, or Chinese celery, depending on your preference and availability.
- Avoid using old, limp, or bitter celery, as they will not dehydrate well and may affect the taste and texture of the final product.

How to prepare

- Wash the celery under cold running water and drain it well. Pat it dry with a paper towel or a clean cloth.

- Cut off the ends and the leaves of the celery and discard them. Cut the stalks into thin slices, using a sharp knife or a mandolin slicer. Try to make the slices as uniform as possible for even drying.
- If you want to add some flavor to your dehydrated celery, you can sprinkle some salt, pepper, garlic powder, parsley, or other seasonings of your choice over the celery slices. Alternatively, you can marinate the celery slices in vinegar, lemon juice, or soy sauce for about an hour before dehydrating them. Do not forget that this option is not suitable for long-term storage.

How to blanch
- Blanching is recommended for dehydrating celery, as it will help retain the natural color and prevent the slices from becoming tough and stringy.
- To blanch celery, bring a large pot of water to a boil and add some salt. Add the celery slices and boil for about 2 minutes, then drain and rinse them under cold water to stop the cooking process.
- Alternatively, you can steam the celery slices for about 4 minutes over boiling water, then cool them under cold water.
- After blanching, pat the celery slices dry with a paper towel or a clean cloth before placing them on dehydrator trays.

Celery chips: Cut the celery stalks into **1/8 inch (0.3 cm)** slices and spread them on the dehydrator trays, after preparing. Set the temperature to **135°F (57°C)** and dry for **6 to 8 hours**, or until the slices are crisp and crunchy. To check for doneness, bite into a slice and see if it breaks easily. You can also bend a slice and see if it cracks. One pound (0.45 kg) of raw celery will yield about **2 cups (60 g)** of celery chips. Celery chips have a mild celery flavor and a light green color. They can be eaten as a snack, or added to soups, salads, and casseroles for extra crunch. They can also be rehydrated by soaking them in water for 15 minutes.

Celery sticks: Cut the celery stalks into **3-inch (7.6 cm)** long and **1/4 inch (0.6 cm)** thick sticks and spread them on the dehydrator trays, after preparing. Set the temperature to **125°F (52°C)** and dry for **10 to 12 hours**, or until the sticks are leathery and chewy. To check for doneness, bend a stick and see if it flexes easily. You can also taste a stick and see if it has a pleasant texture. One pound (0.45 kg) of raw celery will yield about 3 cups (90 g) of celery sticks. Celery sticks have a strong celery flavor and a dark green color. They can be eaten as a healthy snack, or dipped in peanut butter, cream cheese, or hummus for extra protein and flavor. They can also be rehydrated by boiling them in water for 10 minutes.

Celery rings: Cut the celery stalks into 1/2 inch (1.3 cm) thick rings and spread them on the dehydrator trays, after preparing. Set the temperature to 135°F (57°C) and dry for 8 to 10 hours, or until the rings are hard and dry. To check for doneness, tap a ring on a hard surface and see if it makes a sound. You can also squeeze a ring and see if it breaks easily. One pound

(0.45 kg) of raw celery will yield about 2 cups (60 g) of celery rings. Celery rings have a moderate celery flavor and a light green color. They can be used as decoration for cakes, pies, and cupcakes. They can also be added to tea, coffee, or hot chocolate for a refreshing twist.

Cherries

How to choose

- Choose fresh, ripe, and firm cherries with a deep red or purple color and shiny skin. The cherries should be plump and free of bruises, cracks, or insect damage. You can use any variety of cherries, such as Bing, Rainier, or Montmorency, depending on your preference and availability.

- Avoid using unripe, overripe, or spoiled cherries, as they will not dehydrate well and may affect the taste and texture of the final product.

How to prepare

- Wash the cherries under cold running water and drain them well. Pat them dry with a paper towel or a clean cloth.

- Remove the stems and the pits from the cherries with a cherry pitter, a knife, or a paper clip. You can also leave the pits in, but they may affect the flavor and the shelf life of the dehydrated cherries.

- Cut the cherries in half or leave them whole, depending on your preference and the size of the cherries. Cutting the cherries in half will help them dry faster and more evenly, but leaving them whole will retain more juice and flavor.

- Spread the cherries in a single layer on dehydrator trays, leaving some space between them for air circulation. Do not overcrowd the trays, or the cherries will take longer to dry.

How to blanch

- Blanching is not necessary for dehydrating cherries, as they have a low enzyme content and do not brown easily. However, if you want to blanch cherries, you can follow these steps:

- To blanch cherries, bring a large pot of water to a boil and add some lemon juice or vinegar. This will help prevent the cherries from losing their color. Add the cherries and boil for about 1 minute, then drain and rinse them under cold water to stop the cooking process.

- Alternatively, you can steam the cherries for about 2 minutes over boiling water, then cool them under cold water.

- After blanching, pat the cherries dry with a paper towel or a clean cloth before placing them on dehydrator trays.

Cherry halves: Cut the cherries in half and remove the pits. Place them cut-side down on the dehydrator trays after preparing. Set the temperature to **155°F (68°C)** and dry for **12 to 14 hours**. You should get about **1/6 pound (76 g)** of cherry halves from 1 pound (454 g) of raw cherries. To check for doneness, bend a piece and see if it is leathery and not moist. The cherry halves should be dry, firm, and slightly sticky. They have a sweet and sour flavor, a dark red color, and a chewy texture. You can use them as a snack, a garnish, or a rehydrated fruit for pies, cakes, or jams.

Cherry rings: Cut the cherries into thin slices and remove the pits. Place them in a single layer on the dehydrator trays after preparing. Set the temperature to **165°F (74°C)** and dry for **14 to 16 hours**. You should get about **1/10 pound (45 g)** of cherry rings from 1 pound (454 g) of raw cherries. To check for doneness, tear a piece and see if it is dry and not spongy. The cherry rings should be dry, light, and airy. They have a mild and sweet flavor, a light red color, and a crispy texture. You can use them as a snack, a decoration, or a rehydrated fruit for salads, cereals, or smoothies.

Collard greens

How to choose

- Choose fresh, crisp, and dark green collard greens with no signs of wilting, yellowing, or insect damage. The leaves should be tender and the stems should be firm. You can use any variety of collard greens, such as curly, flat, or dinosaur, depending on your preference and availability.
- Avoid using old, tough, or bitter collard greens, as they will not dehydrate well and may affect the taste and texture of the final product.

How to prepare

- Wash the collard greens under cold running water and drain them well. Pat them dry with a paper towel or a clean cloth.
- Cut off the stems and the thick veins from the collard greens and discard them. Cut the leaves into bite-sized pieces, using a sharp knife or kitchen scissors. You can also tear the leaves by hand, but be careful not to bruise them.
- Spread the collard green pieces in a single layer on dehydrator trays, leaving some space between them for air circulation. Do not overcrowd the trays, or the collard greens will take longer to dry.

How to blanch

- Blanching is recommended for dehydrating collard greens, as it will help retain the bright green color and prevent the leaves from becoming tough and leathery.

- To blanch collard greens, bring a large pot of water to a boil and add some salt. Add the collard green pieces and boil for about 2 minutes, then drain and rinse them under cold water to stop the cooking process.

- Alternatively, you can steam the collard green pieces for about 4 minutes over boiling water, then cool them under cold water.

- After blanching, pat the collard green pieces dry with a paper towel or a clean cloth before placing them on dehydrator trays.

Collard green whole leaves or chips: Cut the collard greens into **2-inch (5 cm)** pieces, or leave them whole, discarding the stems. After preparing, toss them with some oil, salt, and your favorite seasonings. Spread them in a single layer on the dehydrator trays. Dehydrate at **125°F (52°C)** for **2 to 4 hours**, or until crisp. Check for doneness by breaking a piece and tasting it. It should be crunchy and flavorful. You can store the chips in an airtight container for up to a week. One pound of raw collard greens will yield about **2 ounces (57 g)** of dried chips. Collard green chips are a healthy and delicious snack that you can enjoy anytime. They have a dark green color and a nutty and savory taste.

Collard green powder: Cut the collard greens into **1-inch (2.5 cm)** pieces, discarding the stems. After preparing, spread them in a single layer on the dehydrator trays. Dehydrate at **95°F (35°C)** for **8 to 10 hours**, or until brittle. Check for doneness by crushing a piece between your fingers. It should crumble easily. Transfer the dried collard greens to a blender or food processor and blend until they turn into a fine powder. You can store the powder in an airtight jar for up to a year. One pound of raw collard greens will yield about **1 ounce (28 g)** of dried powder. Collard green powder is a versatile and nutritious ingredient that you can use to boost the flavor and color of soups, sauces, smoothies, dips, and more. It has a bright green color and a mild and earthy taste.

Corn

How to choose

- Choose fresh, ripe, and tender corn with bright green husks and silky tassels. The kernels should be plump and milky, and the cob should be firm and not dry. You can use any variety of corn, such as yellow, white, or bicolor, depending on your preference and availability.

- Avoid using old, tough, or moldy corn, as they will not dehydrate well and may affect the taste and texture of the final product.

How to prepare

- Remove the husks and the silk from the corn and wash them under cold running water. Dry them with a paper towel or a clean cloth.
- Cut off the kernels from the cob with a sharp knife or a corn stripper. You can also use a food processor or a blender to chop the kernels but be careful not to overprocess them, or they will turn into mush.
- Spread the corn kernels in a single layer on dehydrator trays, leaving some space between them for air circulation. Do not overcrowd the trays, or the corn will take longer to dry.

How to blanch
- Blanching is recommended for dehydrating corn, as it will help retain the natural sweetness and prevent the kernels from becoming hard and chewy.
- To blanch corn, bring a large pot of water to a boil and add some salt. Add the corn kernels and boil for about 4 minutes, then drain and rinse them under cold water to stop the cooking process.
- Alternatively, you can steam the corn kernels for about 6 minutes over boiling water, then cool them under cold water.
- After blanching, pat the corn kernels dry with a paper towel or a clean cloth before placing them on dehydrator trays.

Corn kernels: These are the most common and versatile products of dehydrating corn. To make them, you need to cut the corn off the cob using a sharp knife or a corn stripper. You can cut the kernels as close to the cob as possible, leaving about **1/4 inch (0.6 cm)** of space. After preparing, the kernels should be spread in a single layer on a dehydrator tray, breaking up any large pieces. The drying temperature should be **120°F (49°C)** and the drying time should be **12 to 14 hours**, depending on the humidity level. You can check for doneness by tasting a few kernels. They should be hard and dry, not chewy or moist. One pound (0.45 kg) of raw corn will yield about **1/4 pound (0.11 kg)** of dried corn kernels. Corn kernels can be used in soups, stews, casseroles, salads, and other dishes. They have a sweet and nutty flavor, a bright yellow color, and a crunchy texture. They can also be ground into cornmeal or corn flour for baking.

Corn flour: Cut the corn kernels off the cob and spread them on a dehydrator tray. Prepare it. Dry at **125°F (52°C)** for **6 to 8 hours** until brittle. You will get about **1/3 pound (150 g)** of dried corn flour from 1 pound (454 g) of raw corn. To check for doneness, grind a few kernels in a blender or food processor and see if they turn into a fine powder. Corn flour is useful for making bread, tortillas, muffins, pancakes, and other baked goods. It has a mild and slightly sweet flavor and a pale yellow color.

Cranberries

How to choose

• Choose fresh, ripe, and plump cranberries with a deep red color and a firm texture. The cranberries should bounce when dropped, indicating that they are not soft or rotten. You can also use frozen cranberries, as long as they are not thawed or damaged.

• Avoid using bruised, shriveled, or moldy cranberries, as they will not dehydrate well and may affect the taste and texture of the final product.

How to prepare

• Wash the cranberries under cold running water and drain them well. Pat them dry with a paper towel or a clean cloth.

• Cut the cranberries in half with a sharp knife or a food processor. This will help release some of the juice and make the cranberries easier to dehydrate. You can also pierce the cranberries with a fork or a toothpick, but this may take longer and be less effective.

• If you want to add some sweetness to your dehydrated cranberries, you can soak them in sugar syrup for about an hour before dehydrating them. To make the sugar syrup, dissolve 1 cup of sugar in 2 cups of boiling water and let it cool slightly. Add the cranberries and let them soak, stirring occasionally. Drain the cranberries and pat them dry with a paper towel or a clean cloth.

How to blanch

• Blanching is not necessary for dehydrating cranberries, as they have a low enzyme content and do not brown easily. However, if you want to blanch cranberries, you can follow these steps:

• To blanch cranberries, bring a large pot of water to a boil and add some lemon juice or vinegar. This will help prevent the cranberries from losing their color. Add the cranberries and boil for about 2 minutes, then drain and rinse them under cold water to stop the cooking process.

• Alternatively, you can steam the cranberries for about 3 minutes over boiling water, then cool them under cold water.

• After blanching, pat the cranberries dry with a paper towel or a clean cloth before placing them on dehydrator trays.

Cranberry chips: Cut the cranberries in half about **0.5 inch (1.3 cm)** and place them cut side up on the dehydrator trays. After preparing, dry at **135°F (57°C)** for **8 to 10 hours**, or until crisp and brittle. You should get about **1/4 pound (113 g)** of dried cranberries from 1 pound (454 g) of fresh ones. To check for doneness, break a piece in half and look for any moisture beads. If there are none, the cranberries are done. Cranberry chips are crunchy and tart, with a deep red color. They are great for snacking, adding to granola, or making trail mix.

Cranberry halves: Cut the cranberries in half about **0.5 inch (1.3 cm)** and place them cut side down on the dehydrator trays. After preparing, dry at **130°F (54°C)** for **6 to 8 hours**, or until chewy and leathery. You should get about **1/4 pound (113 g)** of dried cranberries from 1 pound (454 g) of fresh ones. To check for doneness, bite into a cranberry. If it is soft and moist, but not juicy, it is done. Cranberry halves are tender and sour, with a light red color. They are perfect for adding to salads, muffins, cookies, breads, and other recipes that call for dried cranberries.

Cranberry powder: After preparing, dry the cranberries whole at **145°F (63°C)** for **10 to 12 hours**, or until hard and shriveled. You should get about **1/5 pound (91 g)** of dried cranberries from 1 pound (454 g) of fresh ones. To check for doneness, squeeze a cranberry between your fingers. If it feels dry and firm, it is done. Transfer the dried cranberries to a blender or spice grinder and process until they turn into a fine powder. Cranberry powder is tangy and aromatic, with a dark red color. It is a versatile ingredient that can be used to flavor smoothies, yogurt, oatmeal, baked goods, sauces, dressings, and more.

Cucumbers

How to choose

- Choose fresh, firm, and green cucumbers with no signs of wilting, yellowing, or bruising. The skin should be smooth, and the flesh should be crisp and juicy. You can use any variety of cucumbers, such as slicing, pickling, or English cucumbers, depending on your preference and availability.

- Avoid using overripe, soft, or bitter cucumbers, as they will not dehydrate well and may affect the taste and texture of the final product.

How to prepare

- Wash the cucumbers under cold running water and dry them with a paper towel or a clean cloth.

- While cutting, try to make the slices as uniform as possible for even drying.

- If you want to add some flavor to your dehydrated cucumbers, you can sprinkle some salt, pepper, garlic powder, dill, or other seasonings of your choice over the cucumber slices. Alternatively, you can marinate the cucumber slices in vinegar, lemon juice, or soy sauce for about an hour before dehydrating them. Do not forget that this option is not suitable for long-term storage.

How to blanch

Blanching is not necessary for dehydrating cucumbers, as they have a high water content and do not brown easily. However, if you want to blanch cucumbers, you can follow these steps:

- To blanch cucumbers, bring a large pot of water to a boil and add some lemon juice or vinegar. This will help prevent the cucumbers from losing their color. Add the cucumber slices and boil for about 1 minute, then drain and rinse them under cold water to stop the cooking process.

- Alternatively, you can steam the cucumber slices for about 2 minutes over boiling water, then cool them under cold water.

- After blanching, pat the cucumber slices dry with a paper towel or a clean cloth before placing them on dehydrator trays.

Cucumber chips: Cut the cucumbers into thin slices, about **1/8 inch (0.3 cm)** thick. After preparing, sprinkle some salt and vinegar over them for extra flavor. Dehydrate at **135°F (57°C)** for **6 to 8 hours**. You should get about **1/4 cup (15 g)** of dried cucumber chips from 1 pound (454 g) of raw cucumbers. Check for doneness by breaking a chip in half. It should be crisp and dry, not moist or bendable. Cucumber chips are light green and have a tangy and refreshing taste. They are great for snacking or adding to salads and sandwiches.

Cucumber powder: Cut the cucumbers into thin slices, about **1/16 inch   (0.15 cm)** thick. After preparing, dehydrate at **125°F (52°C)** for **8 to 10 hours**. You should get about **2 tablespoons (6 g)** of dried cucumber slices from 1 pound (454 g) of raw cucumbers. Check for doneness by crumbling a slice between your fingers. It should be brittle and powdery, not sticky or chewy. Cucumber powder is pale green and has a mild and fresh flavor. You can use it to make cucumber water, smoothies, dips, dressings, soups, or facial masks.

Cucumber jerky: Cut the cucumbers into thick strips, about **1/4 inch (0.6 cm)** thick and **3 inch (7.6 cm)** long. After preparing, marinate them in a mixture of soy sauce, honey, garlic, ginger, and red pepper flakes for at least **2 hours**. Dehydrate at **145°F (63°C)** for **10 to 12 hours**. You should get about **1/3 cup (20 g)** of dried cucumber jerky from 1 pound (454 g) of raw cucumbers. Check for doneness by bending a strip. It should be leathery and pliable, not soft or brittle. Cucumber jerky is dark brown and has a savory and spicy flavor. It is a protein-rich and low-carb snack that can satisfy your hunger and cravings.

How to choose

Choose fresh, ripe, and firm dragon fruits with bright and even skin color. The skin should be slightly soft to the touch, but not mushy or wrinkled. The flesh should be juicy and sweet, with tiny black seeds. You can use either red or white-fleshed dragon fruits, depending on your preference and availability.

Avoid using unripe, overripe, or damaged dragon fruits, as they will not dehydrate well and may affect the taste and texture of the final product.

How to prepare

- Wash the dragon fruit under cold running water and dry it with a paper towel or a clean cloth.
- Cut off the stem and the bottom of the dragon fruit and discard them. Cut the dragon fruit in half and scoop out the flesh with a spoon. You can also peel off the skin with a knife or a vegetable peeler, but be careful not to waste too much flesh.
- While cutting, try to make the slices as uniform as possible for drying.

How to blanch

Blanching is not necessary for dehydrating dragon fruit, as it has a low enzyme content and does not brown easily. However, if you want to blanch dragon fruit, you can follow these steps:

- To blanch dragon fruit, bring a large pot of water to a boil and add some lemon juice or vinegar. This will help prevent the dragon fruit from losing its color. Add the dragon fruit slices and boil for about 1 minute, then drain and rinse them under cold water to stop the cooking process.
- Alternatively, you can steam the dragon fruit slices for about 2 minutes over boiling water, then cool them under cold water.
- After blanching, pat the dragon fruit slices dry with a paper towel or a clean cloth before placing them on dehydrator trays.

Dragon fruit cubes: Cut the dragon fruit into small cubes, about **1/2 inch (1.3 cm)** on each side. After preparing, place them on the dehydrator trays in a single layer, leaving some space between them. Set the dehydrator to **135°F (57°C)** and dry for **10 to 12 hours,** or until the cubes are shriveled and chewy. You should get about **1/5 pound (91 g)** of dried cubes from 1 pound (454 g) of fresh dragon fruit. To check for doneness, squeeze a cube with your fingers and make sure it is not mushy or juicy. Dragon fruit cubes have a chewy and dense texture, a sweet and sour flavor, and a dark pink or white color. They are like dried cranberries or raisins and can be used in the same way. You can add them to salads, oatmeal, trail mix, or cereal, or eat them as a snack.

Dragon fruit chips: Cut the dragon fruit into thin slices, about **1/8 inch (0.3 cm)** thick. After preparing, place them on the dehydrator trays in a single layer, leaving some space between them. Set the dehydrator to **135°F (57°C)** and dry for **6 to 8 hours,** or until crisp. You should get about **1/4 pound (113 g)** of dried chips from 1 pound (454 g) of fresh dragon fruit. To check for doneness, break a chip in half and look for any moisture beads. The chips should be dry and crunchy, not sticky or chewy. Dragon fruit chips have a sweet and tangy flavor, a bright pink or white color, and a crispy texture. They are great for snacking, adding to granola, or topping yogurt or ice cream.

Dragon fruit candies: Cut the dragon fruit into small pieces, about **1/4 inch   (0.6 cm)** on each side. After preparing, place them in a bowl and sprinkle some honey over them. Toss them well to coat them evenly. You can also add some lemon juice, vanilla extract, or cinnamon for extra flavor if you like. Place the pieces on the dehydrator trays in a single layer, leaving some space between them. Set the dehydrator to **145°F (63°C)** and dry for **12 to 14 hours,** or until the pieces are chewy and sticky. You should get about **1/6 pound (76 g)** of dried candies from 1 pound (454 g) of fresh dragon fruit. To check for doneness, bite into a piece and make sure it is not hard or crunchy. Dragon fruit candies have a sweet and tangy flavor, a bright pink or white color, and a chewy and sticky texture. They are like gummy bears or fruit snacks and can be enjoyed as a treat or a dessert.

Eggplant

How to choose

- Choose fresh, firm, and smooth eggplants with no bruises, cuts, or soft spots. The skin should be glossy, and the stem should be green. The size and shape of the eggplant do not matter, as long as it is ripe and not overgrown.

- Avoid using old, wrinkled, or bitter eggplants, as they will not dehydrate well and may affect the taste and texture of the final product.

How to prepare

- Wash the eggplant under cold running water and dry it with a paper towel or a clean cloth.

- Cut off the stem and the bottom of the eggplant and discard them. Cut the eggplant into thin slices or cubes. Try to make the pieces as uniform as possible for even drying.

- Sprinkle some salt over the eggplant slices and let them sit for about 15 minutes. This will help draw out some of the moisture and bitterness from the eggplant. Rinse the salt off the eggplant slices and pat them dry with a paper towel or a clean cloth.

How to blanch

- Blanching is recommended for dehydrating eggplant, as it will help prevent browning and improve the quality of the dehydrated product.

- To blanch eggplant, bring a large pot of water to a boil and add some lemon juice or vinegar. This will help prevent the eggplant from turning brown. Add the eggplant slices and boil for about 2 minutes, then drain and rinse them under cold water to stop the cooking process.

- Alternatively, you can sprinkle some salt and vinegar on both sides of the slices and let them sit for 15 minutes. This will help to draw out the moisture and enhance the flavor.
- Pat the eggplant slices dry with a paper towel or a clean cloth before placing them on dehydrator trays.

Eggplant chips: Cut the eggplant into thin slices, about **1/8 inch (3 mm)** thick. After preparing, arrange them in a single layer on the dehydrator trays and set the temperature to **135°F (57°C)**. Dehydrate for **6 to 8 hours**, or until crisp. Check for doneness by breaking a chip in half. It should snap easily and have no moisture inside. Eggplant chips are a crunchy and healthy snack that can be enjoyed plain or with your favorite dip. They have a light brown color and a tangy taste. You can also season them with herbs, spices, or cheese for more variety. You can get about **1/4 pound (113 g)** of dried chips from 1 pound (454 g) of raw eggplant.

Eggplant jerky: Cut the eggplant into thin strips, about **1/4 inch (6 mm)** thick and **4 inch (10 cm)** long. After preparing, marinate them in a mixture of soy sauce, honey, garlic, ginger, and red pepper flakes for at least 2 hours, or overnight. Drain the excess marinade and place the strips on the dehydrator trays. Set the temperature to **145°F (63°C)** and dehydrate for **8 to 10 hours**, or until chewy. Check for doneness by bending a strip. It should be flexible but not brittle. Eggplant jerky is a savory and satisfying snack that can be eaten as is or added to salads, sandwiches, or stir-fries. It has a dark brown color and a sweet and spicy flavor. You can also experiment with different marinades to suit your taste. You can get about **1/5 pound (91 g)** of dried jerky from 1 pound (454 g) of raw eggplant.

Eggplant cubes: Cut the eggplant into small cubes, about **1/4 inch (6 mm)** in size. After blanching, spread the cubes on the dehydrator trays and set the temperature to **130°F (54°C)**. Dehydrate for **8 to 10 hours**, or until dry and hard. Check for doneness by biting into a cube. It should be crunchy and have no moisture inside. Eggplant cubes are a handy ingredient that can be rehydrated and used in soups, casseroles, curries, or salads. They have a light purple color and a neutral taste. You can also season them with salt, pepper, or herbs before dehydrating them for more flavor. You can get about **1/8 pound (57 g)** of dried cubes from 1 pound (454 g) of raw eggplant.

Figs

How to Choose

- The best figs for dehydrating are ripe, juicy, and firm. Avoid figs that are too soft, mushy, or have mold or bruises, as they may be spoiled or overripe.
- You can use any variety of figs for dehydrating, such as black, green, or purple figs. Each variety has a different color, flavor, and sweetness level, so you can experiment and find your favorite.

- You can use fresh or frozen figs for dehydrating, but fresh figs will have more flavor and juice. If you use frozen figs, thaw them completely and pat them dry before dehydrating.

How to Prepare

- Wash the figs under cold running water and gently rub them to remove any dirt or dust. Pat them dry with a clean towel or paper towel.
- Remove the stems from the figs with a sharp knife. You can also peel the skin if you don't like the texture or taste, but the skin contains valuable nutrients and fiber.
- Cut the figs into your desired shape and size. Try to make the pieces as uniform as possible.
- Optional, place the figs in a large bowl and toss them with some olive oil, salt, honey, or other seasonings of your choice. This will help enhance the flavor and prevent the figs from sticking to the dehydrator trays.

How to Blanch

- Blanching is an optional step that can help preserve the color, and texture of the figs.
- To blanch figs, bring a large pot of water to a boil and add some lemon juice or citric acid.
- Add the figs to the boiling water in batches and cook for about 1 minute, or until they turn slightly translucent. Do not overcook them, as they will become mushy and lose their shape.
- Drain the figs and immediately transfer them to a large bowl of ice water to cool them down and stop the cooking process. Drain them again and pat them dry with a towel or paper towel.

Whole Figs: Cut off the stems and make a small slit on the bottom of each fig. After preparing, place them on the dehydrator trays with some space between them. Set the temperature to **115°F (46°C)** and dry for **18 to 24 hours**. You will get about **1/5 pound (90 g)** of dried whole figs from 1 pound (454 g) of fresh figs. Check for doneness by squeezing a fig gently; it should be firm but not hard. Whole figs are sweet and juicy, with a dark purple color and a soft texture. They are wonderful for stuffing with cheese, nuts, or chocolate, or for making fig pudding or cake.

Figs Halves: Cut the figs in half and place them on the dehydrator trays with the cut side up. After preparing, set the temperature to **135°F (57°C)** and dry for **8 to 12 hours**. You will get about **1/4 pound (113 g)** of dried fig halves from 1 pound (454 g) of fresh figs. Check for doneness by squeezing a fig half gently; it should be pliable but not sticky or moist. Figs halves are sweet and chewy, with a dark brown color and a wrinkled appearance. They are great for snacking, baking, or adding to granola or trail mix.

Figs Slices: Cut the figs into thin slices, about **1/4 inch (6 mm)** thick. After preparing, arrange them on the dehydrator trays in a single layer. Set the temperature to **125°F (52°C)** and dry for **6 to 10 hours**. You will get about **1/5 pound (90 g)** of dried fig slices from 1 pound (454 g) of fresh figs. Check for doneness by bending a fig slice; it should be leathery, but not brittle. Figs slices are sweet and tender, with a light brown color and a smooth texture. They are perfect for topping yogurt, oatmeal, or salads, or making fig bars or jam.

Figs Chips: Cut the figs into very thin slices, about **1/8 inch (3 mm)** thick. After preparing, arrange them on the dehydrator trays in a single layer. Set the temperature to **145°F (63°C)** and dry for **4 to 6 hours**. You will get about **1/6 pound (75 g)** of dried fig chips from 1 pound (454 g) of fresh figs. Check for doneness by breaking a fig chip; it should be crisp and crunchy. Figs chips are sweet and crispy, with a dark brown color and a brittle texture. They are delicious for munching, dipping, or making fig candy or brittle.

Garlic

How to Choose

- The best garlic for dehydrating are fresh, firm, and plump bulbs that have no signs of sprouting, mold, or damage. Avoid garlic that is soft, shriveled, or green shoots, as they may have lost some of their flavor and quality.

- You can use any variety of garlic for dehydrating, such as white, purple, or elephant garlic. Each variety has a different size, shape, and taste, so you can experiment and find your favorite.

- You can use fresh or frozen garlic for dehydrating, but fresh garlic will have more flavor and aroma. If you use frozen garlic, thaw it completely and pat it dry before dehydrating.

- You can dehydrate whole garlic cloves, sliced garlic, minced garlic, or crushed garlic, depending on your preference and the intended use. Whole cloves will retain more of their natural oils and flavor, while sliced, minced, or crushed garlic will dehydrate faster and be easier to grind into powder or flakes.

How to Prepare

- Peel the garlic cloves by hand or use a garlic peeler, which is a silicone tube that can remove the skin by rolling the cloves inside it. You can also smash the cloves with the flat side of a knife to loosen the skin and then peel it off.

- Cut the garlic into your desired shape and size with a knife, a mandolin slicer, a food processor, or a garlic press. Try to make the pieces as uniform as possible for drying.

- Place the garlic in a large bowl and toss them with some olive oil, salt, or other seasonings of your choice. This will help prevent the garlic from sticking to the dehydrator trays and enhance the flavor.

How to Blanch

- Blanching is an optional step that can help preserve the color, texture, and nutritional value of the garlic. Blanching involves briefly boiling the garlic in water and then plunging it into ice water to stop the cooking process.

- To blanch garlic, bring a large pot of water to a boil and add some lemon juice or vinegar. This will help prevent the garlic from browning and losing vitamin C during the drying process.

- Add the garlic to the boiling water in batches and cook for about 30 seconds, or until they turn slightly translucent. Do not overcook them, as they will become mushy and lose their shape.

- Drain the garlic and immediately transfer them to a large bowl of ice water to cool them down and stop the cooking process. Drain them again and pat them dry with a towel or paper towel.

Garlic powder: To make garlic powder, peel and slice the garlic cloves into thin slices, about **1/8 inch (3 mm)** thick. Spread them evenly on the dehydrator trays and dry at **125°F (52°C)** for **6 to 8 hours**. You should get about **1/4 cup (30 g)** of dried garlic slices from **1 pound (454 g)** of raw garlic. To check for doneness, the slices should be crisp and brittle, and easily crumble when pressed. To make garlic powder, you need to grind the dried slices in a blender or food processor until they reach a fine consistency. You can also add some salt or other spices to enhance the flavor. Garlic powder has a light tan color and a strong garlic aroma. It has a mild and slightly sweet garlic flavor that is suitable for many dishes. You can use garlic powder as a seasoning for soups, sauces, meats, vegetables, and more.

Garlic flakes: To make garlic flakes, peel and chop the garlic cloves into small pieces, about **1/4 inch (6 mm)** in size. Spread them evenly on the dehydrator trays and dry at **135°F (57°C)** for **8 to 10 hours**. You should get about **1/3 cup (40 g)** of dried garlic pieces from **1 pound (454 g)** of raw garlic. To check for doneness, the pieces should be hard and dry, and not sticky or moist. Garlic flakes have a golden brown color and a pungent garlic aroma. They have a strong and spicy garlic flavor that adds a kick to any dish. You can use garlic flakes as a substitute for fresh garlic in recipes that require cooking, such as stews, casseroles, curries, and more.

Garlic chips: To make garlic chips, peel and slice the garlic cloves into thin rounds, about **1/16 inch (1.5 mm)** thick. Spread them evenly on the dehydrator trays and dry at **145°F (63°C)** for **4 to 6 hours**. You should get about **1/2 cup (60 g)** of dried garlic rounds from **1 pound (454 g)** of raw garlic. To check for doneness, the rounds should be crisp and crunchy, and not bend or break. Garlic chips have a dark brown color and a smoky garlic aroma. They have a rich and savory garlic flavor that makes them a great snack or garnish. You can use garlic chips as a crunchy topping for salads, soups, pizzas, and more. You can also eat them plain or dip them in your favorite sauce. Garlic chips can be stored in an airtight container for up to a year.

Garlic granules: To make garlic granules, peel and mince the garlic cloves into tiny pieces, about **1/16 inch (1.5 mm)** or smaller. Spread them evenly on the dehydrator trays and dry at **155°F (68°C)** for **10 to 12 hours**. You should get about **3/4 cup (90 g)** of dried garlic bits from **1 pound (454 g)** of raw garlic. To check for doneness, the bits should be hard and dry, and not sticky or moist. Garlic granules have a light brown color and a fresh garlic aroma. They have a moderate and balanced garlic flavor that is versatile and easy to use. You can use garlic granules as a seasoning for meats, poultry, fish, vegetables, and more. You can also mix them with butter, oil, or cheese to make a delicious spread or dip.

Grapefruits

How to Choose

- The best grapefruit for dehydrating are ripe, juicy, and sweet. Avoid grapefruit that are too soft, wrinkled, or have brown spots, as they may be overripe or spoiled.

- You can use any variety of grapefruit for dehydration, such as white, pink, red, or ruby. Each variety has a different color, flavor, and sweetness level, so you can experiment and find your favorite.

- You can use fresh or frozen grapefruit for dehydrating, but fresh grapefruit will have more flavor and juice. If you use frozen grapefruit, thaw it completely and pat it dry before dehydrating.

- You can dehydrate whole grapefruit slices, or cut them into smaller pieces, depending on your preference and the size of your dehydrator trays. Smaller pieces will dehydrate faster and be easier to eat, while larger slices will retain more juice and flavor.

How to Prepare

- Wash the grapefruit under cold running water and scrub them gently to remove any dirt or wax. Pat them dry with a clean towel or paper towel.

- Cut off the stem and blossom ends of the grapefruit with a sharp knife. You can also peel off the skin if you don't like the bitter taste, but the skin contains valuable nutrients and fiber.

- Cut the grapefruit into 1/4-inch thick slices or smaller pieces with a knife, a mandolin slicer, or a food processor. Try to make the slices or pieces as uniform as possible for even drying.

- Place the grapefruit in a large bowl and toss them with some olive oil, salt, honey, or other seasonings of your choice. This will help enhance the flavor and prevent the grapefruit from sticking to the dehydrator trays.

How to Blanch

- Blanching is an optional step that can help preserve the color, texture, and vitamin C content of the grapefruit. Blanching involves briefly boiling the grapefruit in water and then plunging them into ice water to stop the cooking process.

- To blanch grapefruit, bring a large pot of water to a boil and add some lemon juice or citric acid. This will help prevent the grapefruit from browning and losing vitamin C during the drying process.

- Add the grapefruit to the boiling water in batches and cook for about 1 minute, or until they turn slightly translucent. Do not overcook them, as they will become mushy and lose their shape.

- Drain the grapefruit and immediately transfer them to a large bowl of ice water to cool them down and stop the cooking process. Drain them again and pat them dry with a towel or paper towel.

- Proceed with seasoning and dehydrating the grapefruit as usual.

Grapefruit chips: Cut the grapefruit into thin slices, about **1/8 inch (3 mm)** thick. Remove any seeds and excess membrane. Place the slices on dehydrator trays and dry at **135°F (57°C)** for **8 to 10 hours**, or until crisp and leathery. One pound (454 g) of raw grapefruit will yield about **2 ounces (57 g)** of dried chips. Check for doneness by breaking a slice in half; there should be no moisture beads. Grapefruit chips are tangy and sweet, with a bright orange or pink color and a chewy texture. They make a great snack on their own, or you can dip them in chocolate, yogurt, or nut butter for a more decadent treat.

Grapefruit powder: To make grape powder, you need to follow the same steps as grape chips but dry them for a longer time, about **12 to 14 hours** until they are very crisp and brittle. One pound (454 g) of raw grapefruit will yield about **1.5 ounces (43 g)** of dried pieces. Check for doneness by crushing a piece with your fingers; it should crumble easily. Transfer the dried pieces to a blender or food processor and grind them into a fine powder. Grapefruit powder is sour and aromatic, with a pale yellow or pink color and a powdery texture. You can use it to flavor drinks, smoothies, desserts, sauces, marinades, or salad dressings. You can also sprinkle it on salads, fruits, or yogurt for a zesty boost.

Grapefruit zest: Peel the grapefruit and remove the white pith. Cut the peel into thin strips or use a zester to grate it. Place the zest on dehydrator trays and dry at **95°F (35°C)** for **2 to 4 hours**, or until dry and crisp. One pound (454 g) of raw grapefruit will yield about **0.5 oz (14 g)** of dried zest. Check for doneness by rubbing a piece of zest between your fingers; it should crumble easily. Grapefruit zest is bitter and fragrant, with a bright orange or pink color and a hard texture. You can use it to add flavor and color to baked goods, candies, teas, cocktails, or dishes. You can also mix it with salt, sugar, or spices to make your seasoning blends.

Grapefruit candy: Cut the grapefruit into wedges, about **1/2 inch (12 mm)** thick. Remove any seeds and excess membrane. Place the wedges in a saucepan and cover them with water. Bring to a boil, then reduce the heat and simmer for 15 minutes. Drain the wedges and return them to the saucepan. Add enough sugar to cover them and bring to a boil again. Simmer for 15 minutes, then drain the wedges and place them on dehydrator trays. Dry at **140°F (60°C)** for **12 to 14 hours**, or until dry and sticky. One pound (454 g) of raw grapefruit will yield about **4 ounces (113 g)** of dried candy. Check for doneness by tasting a piece of candy; it should be sweet and chewy. Grapefruit candy is sugary and tangy, with a bright orange or pink color and a sticky texture. You can enjoy it as a sweet treat, or coat it with sugar, chocolate, or nuts for a more indulgent snack.

Grapes

How to choose

The best grapes for dehydration are fresh, ripe, and juicy. They should have a smooth skin and a firm flesh. Avoid grapes that are green, wrinkled, bruised, or have soft spots.

You can use any variety of grapes, such as red, green, or black, depending on your preference and availability. Each variety has a slightly different flavor, sweetness, and color. Red grapes are tarter and tangier, green grapes are milder and sweeter, and black grapes are richer and more intense.

How to prepare

Wash the grapes thoroughly under running water, and remove any dirt or insects. You can also soak them in a solution of water and vinegar for 15 minutes to disinfect them and remove any residue.

Remove the grapes from the stems, and discard them. You can also cut the grapes in half, if you prefer, to speed up the drying process and reduce the size of the raisins.

Pierce the skin of each grape with a knife, a fork, or a toothpick. This will help the moisture escape and prevent the grapes from bursting during dehydration. You can also blanch the grapes in boiling water for 30 seconds, and then plunge them into ice water to stop the cooking process. This will also crack the skin and preserve the color of the grapes.

How to blanch

Blanching is an optional step. To blanch the grapes in water, bring a large pot of water to a boil, and add a pinch of salt and a splash of lemon juice. This can help keep the grapes bright and fresh. Add the grapes in batches, and boil them for about 30 seconds. Then, transfer them to a bowl of ice water, and drain them well.

To blanch the grapes in a sugar syrup, combine 4 cups of water and 2 cups of sugar in a large pot, and bring it to a boil. Stir until the sugar dissolves, and add a splash of lemon juice. This can help enhance the flavor and sweetness of the grapes. Add the grapes in batches, and simmer them for about 5 minutes. Then, transfer them to a bowl of ice water, and drain them well.

Blanching can help prevent the grapes from browning or losing their flavor during dehydration. However, it can also make them softer and stickier, and add extra sugar to the final product. You can skip this step if you prefer, or experiment with different blanching times and methods to find your preferred result.

Raisins: To make raisins, you need to cut the grapes in half and remove the seeds if any. Place them cut-side up on the dehydrator trays and dry at **130°F (54°C)** for **18 to 24 hours**. You will get about **1/2 pound (230 g)** of raisins from 1 pound (454 g) of grapes. To check for doneness, squeeze a few raisins between your fingers. They should be pliable and wrinkled, but not sticky or hard. Raisins are sweet and chewy, with a dark brown color. They are great for snacking, baking, or adding to cereals, salads, and trail mixes.

Grape Chips: To make grape chips, you need to slice the grapes thinly, about **1/8 inch (3 mm)** thick. Arrange them in a single layer on the dehydrator trays and dry them at **135°F (57°C)** for **10 to 12 hours**, flipping them halfway through. You will get about **1/8 pound (57 g)** of grape chips from 1 pound (454 g) of grapes. To check for doneness, take a few chips out and let them cool. They should be crisp and brittle, with no moisture left. Grape chips are crunchy and tart, with a light purple color. They are a fun and healthy alternative to potato chips and can be enjoyed as a snack or sprinkled over yogurt, ice cream, or oatmeal.

Grape Powder: To make grape powder, you need to follow the same steps as grape chips but dry them for a longer time, about **12 to 14 hours** until they are very crisp and brittle. You will get about **1/10 pound (45 g)** of grape powder from 1 pound (454 g) of grapes. To check for doneness, break a few chips in half and look for any moisture beads. They should be completely dry and snap easily. Grape powder is fine and powdery, with a light purple color. It has a concentrated grape flavor and can be used to add sweetness and color to smoothies, drinks, desserts, or sauces.

Green beans

How to choose

The best green beans for dehydration are fresh, crisp, and tender. They should have a bright green color and a firm texture. Avoid green beans that are yellow, wilted, or have holes or spots.

You can use any variety of green beans, such as string, snap, or French, depending on your preference and availability. Each variety has a slightly different flavor, shape, and size. String beans have a thin and long pod with a string along the seam. Snap beans have a thicker and shorter pod that snaps easily. French beans have a flat and slender pod that is more delicate and sweet.

How to prepare

Wash the green beans thoroughly under running water, and remove any dirt or insects. You can also soak them in a solution of water and vinegar for 15 minutes to sanitize them and remove any residue.

Cut or snap the ends off the green beans, and discard them. You can also remove the strings from the string beans if you prefer. Some people like to keep the strings on, as they add texture and flavor to the final product.

Dry the green beans well in a salad spinner or by gently patting them with a clean towel. Excess moisture can prevent the green beans from drying evenly and quickly.

How to blanch

Blanching is an optional step that can help preserve the color, flavor, and nutrients of the green beans. It involves briefly boiling the green beans in water or a salt solution, and then plunging them into ice water to stop the cooking process.

To blanch the green beans in water, bring a large pot of water to a boil, and add a pinch of baking soda. This can help keep the green beans green and bright. Add the green beans in batches, and boil them for about 1 minute. Then, transfer them to a bowl of ice water, and drain them well.

To blanch the green beans in a salt solution, dissolve 1/4 cup of salt in 4 cups of water in a large pot, and bring it to a boil. This can help enhance the flavor and texture of the green beans. Add the green beans in batches, and boil them for about 2 minutes. Then, transfer them to a bowl of ice water, and drain them well.

Blanching can help prevent the green beans from browning or losing their flavor during dehydration. However, it can also make them softer and less crunchy, and add extra salt or sodium to the final product. You can skip this step if you prefer, or experiment with different blanching times and methods to find your preferred result.

Green bean whole or pieces: Wash and trim the green beans and cut them into small pieces, about **1/2 inch (12 mm)** in size, or leave them **whole**. Blanch the pieces in boiling water for **3 minutes** and then plunge them into ice water to stop the cooking process. Drain the pieces and spread them on the dehydrator trays in a single layer. Set the temperature to **125°F (52°C)** and dry for **8 to 10 hours**, or until the pieces are dry and hard. Check for doneness by breaking a piece with your fingers; it should snap easily and not feel moist. Green bean pieces have a mild and nutty green bean flavor and aroma, with a crunchy texture. They have a dark green color and a round shape. You can use them to add flavor and texture to soups, stews, casseroles, or salads. You can also rehydrate them by soaking them in water or broth for about 20 minutes. One pound of fresh green beans will yield about 4 **ounces (113 g)** of dried green bean pieces.

Green bean powder: Repeat all the steps for green bean pieces. Transfer the dried strips to a blender or a spice grinder and process them into a fine powder. Green bean powder has a concentrated and fresh green bean flavor and aroma, with a slight bitterness. It has a light green color and a fine texture. You can use it to add flavor and color to smoothies, juices, sauces, dips, or rubs. You can also mix it with salt, pepper, garlic, and onion to make your green bean seasoning. One pound of fresh green beans will yield about **3 ounces (85 g)** of dried green bean powder.

Guava

How to choose

The best guava for dehydration is ripe, firm, and juicy. They should have green to yellow skin and pink to white flesh. Avoid guava that are overripe, mushy, or have bruises or spots. You can use any variety of guava, such as common, apple, lemon, or strawberry, depending on your preference and availability. Each variety has a slightly different flavor, sweetness, and size.

How to prepare

- Wash the guava thoroughly under running water, and peel them with a knife or a peeler. You can also leave the skin on, as it contains fiber and antioxidants, but it may be tougher and bitter than the flesh.

- Cut the guava into thin slices, depending on preferences. Try to make the slices as even and uniform as possible, so that they dry at the same rate. You can also cut the guava into wedges or cubes if you prefer.

- Remove any seeds from the slices, as they can add bitterness or hardness to the final product. You can use a toothpick or a small knife to pry them out or scoop them out with a spoon.

How to blanch

- Blanching is an optional step. To blanch the guava in water, bring a large pot of water to a boil, and add a pinch of salt and a splash of lemon juice. This can help keep the guava bright and fresh. Add the guava slices in batches, and boil them for about 30 seconds. Then, transfer them to a bowl of ice water, and drain them well.

- To blanch the guava in a sugar syrup, combine 4 cups of water and 2 cups of sugar in a large pot, and bring it to a boil. Stir until the sugar dissolves, and add a splash of lemon juice. This can help enhance the flavor and sweetness of the guava. Add the guava slices in batches, and simmer them for about 5 minutes. Then, transfer them to a bowl of ice water, and drain them well.

- Blanching can help prevent the guava from browning or losing its flavor during dehydration. However, it can also make them softer and stickier, and add extra sugar to the final product. You can skip this step if you prefer, or experiment with different blanching times and methods to find your preferred result.

Guava slices: Cut the guava into thin slices, about **1/8 inch (3 mm)** thick. You can peel the guava or leave the skin on, depending on your preference. Remove any seeds and spread the slices on the dehydrator trays in a single layer. Set the temperature to **135°F (57°C)** and dry for **6 to 10 hours**, or until the slices are dry and leathery. Check for doneness by bending a slice; it should be flexible and not sticky. Guava slices are chewy and sweet, with a tropical guava flavor and aroma. They have a light pink or green color and a flat shape. You can enjoy them as a snack, use them as a topping for yogurt, cereal, or ice cream, or rehydrate them and use them as a filling for pies, cakes, or pastries. 1 pound of fresh guava will yield about **4 ounces (113 g)** of dried guava slices.

Guava chips: Cut the guava into thick slices, about **1/4 inch (6 mm)** thick. You can peel the guava or leave the skin on, depending on your preference. Remove any seeds, sprinkle some honey, cinnamon, and nutmeg over the slices and toss to coat. Spread the slices on the dehydrator trays in a single layer. Set the temperature to **145°F (63°C)** and dry for **10 to 12 hours**, or until the slices are crisp and crunchy. Check for doneness by biting into a slice; it should not be chewy or moist. Guava chips are crispy and sweet, with a spicy guava flavor and aroma. They have a golden brown color and a round shape. You can enjoy them as a snack, or serve them with whipped cream, custard, or chocolate sauce. 1 pound of fresh guava will yield about **5 ounces (142 g)** of dried guava chips.

Guava jerky: Cut the guava into thin strips, about **1/4 inch (6 mm)** wide. You can peel the guava or leave the skin on, depending on your preference. Remove any seeds and place the strips in a large bowl. Let them dry and then add **1 ounce (300 g)** of honey and **1** vanilla **tube.** Marinate for about 5 hours. Place them on the dehydrator trays in a single layer. Set the temperature to **140°F (60°C)** and dry for **10 to 12 hours**, or until the strips are dry and chewy. Check for doneness by bending a strip; it should not break easily and not feel moist. Guava jerky is sweet, with a chewy and meaty texture. It has a dark brown color and a flat shape. You can enjoy it as a snack, or use it as a protein source for hiking, camping, or traveling. 1 pound of fresh guava will yield about **4 ounces (113 g)** of dried guava jerky.

Guava powder: Repeat all the steps for guava chips. Transfer the dried pieces to a blender or a spice grinder and process them into a fine powder. Guava powder has a concentrated and fruity guava flavor and scent, with a slight acidity. It has a light pink or green color and a fine texture. You can use it to add flavor and color to smoothies, juices, lemonades, sauces, dressings, or marinades. You can also mix it with sugar, salt, and spices to make your guava seasoning. 1 pound of fresh guava will yield about **3 ounces (85 g)** of dried guava powder.

Kale

How to choose

- The best kale for dehydration is fresh, crisp, and tender. They should have a dark green color and a firm texture. Avoid kale that is yellow, wilted, or has holes or spots.
- You can use any variety of kale, such as curly, red, or baby kale, depending on your preference and availability. Each variety has a slightly different flavor, texture, and shape. Curly kale is the most common and has a curly and frilly edge. Lacinato kale is also known as dinosaur or Tuscan kale and is flat and long. Red kale has a reddish-purple stem and vein. Baby kale is smaller and more tender than mature kale.

How to prepare

- Wash the kale thoroughly under running water, and remove any dirt or insects. You can also soak them in a solution of water and vinegar for 15 minutes to sanitize them and remove any residue.
- You don't need to remove the stems, as they will become crispy and edible after dehydration. However, you can trim them if they are too thick or tough.
- Dry the kale well in a salad spinner or by gently patting them with a clean towel. Excess moisture can prevent the kale from drying evenly and quickly.

How to blanch

- Blanching is an optional step that can help preserve the color, flavor, and nutrients of the kale. It involves briefly boiling the kale in water or a salt solution, and then plunging them into ice water to stop the cooking process.
- To blanch the kale in water, bring a large pot of water to a boil, and add a pinch of baking soda. This can help keep the kale green and bright. Add the kale in batches, and boil them for about 1 minute. Then, transfer them to a bowl of ice water, and drain them well.
- To blanch the kale in a salt solution, dissolve 1/4 cup of salt in 4 cups of water in a large pot, and bring it to a boil. This can help enhance the flavor and texture of the kale. Add the kale in batches, and boil them for about 2 minutes. Then, transfer them to a bowl of ice water, and drain them well.
- Blanching can help prevent the kale from browning or losing its flavor during dehydration. However, it can also make them softer and less crispy, and add extra salt or sodium to the final product. You can skip this step if you prefer, or experiment with different blanching times and methods to find your preferred result.

Kale flakes or whole leaves: Wash and dry the kale and remove the stems. Tear the leaves into small pieces, about **1 inch (25 mm)** in size, or you can use whole leaves depending on preferences. Spread the pieces on the dehydrator trays in a single layer. Set the temperature to **95°F (35°C)** and dry for **2 to 4 hours**, or until the pieces are dry and crisp. Check for doneness by crushing a piece with your fingers; it should crumble easily and not feel moist. Kale flakes have a mild and earthy kale flavor and aroma, with a crunchy texture. They have a dark green color and a flaky shape. You can use them to add flavor and texture to soups, salads, sandwiches, or wraps. You can also rehydrate them by soaking them in water for about 10 minutes.

Kale powder: Wash and dry the kale and remove the stems. Cut the leaves into thin strips, about **1/4 inch (6 mm)** wide. Spread the strips on the dehydrator trays in a single layer. Set the temperature to **95°F (35°C)** and dry for **4 to 6 hours**, or until the strips are dry and brittle. Check for doneness by breaking a strip with your fingers; it should snap easily and not feel sticky. Transfer the dried strips to a blender or a spice grinder and process them into a fine powder. Kale powder has a concentrated and fresh kale flavor and aroma, with a slight bitterness. It has a light green color and a fine texture. You can use it to add flavor and color to smoothies, juices, dressings, dips, or sauces. You can also mix it with salt, pepper, garlic, and onion to make your kale seasoning.

Kiwis

How to choose

The best kiwi for dehydration are ripe, firm, and juicy. They should have bright green flesh and smooth brown skin. Avoid kiwi that are overripe, mushy, or have soft spots.

You can use any variety of kiwi, such as Hayward, Gold, or Zespri, depending on your preference and availability. Each variety has a slightly different flavor, sweetness, and size. Hayward kiwis are the most common and have a tart and tangy taste. Gold kiwi are sweeter and have yellow flesh. Zespri kiwi are smaller and have a sweeter and milder taste.

How to prepare

Wash the kiwi thoroughly under running water, and scrub them with a brush or a sponge to remove any dirt or fuzz. You can also peel the kiwi with a knife or a spoon if you prefer. Some people like to keep the skin on, as it adds fiber and texture to the final product. Cut the kiwi and try to make the slices as even and uniform as possible, so that they dry at the same rate. Remove any seeds or white cores from the slices, as they can add bitterness or hardness to the final product. You can use a toothpick or a small knife to pry them out.

How to blanch

Blanching is an optional step. To blanch the kiwi in water, bring a large pot of water to a boil, and add a pinch of salt and a splash of lemon juice. Add the kiwi slices in batches, and boil them for about 30 seconds. Then, transfer them to a bowl of ice water, and drain them well.

Blanching can help prevent the kiwi from browning or losing their flavor during dehydration. However, it can also make them softer and stickier, and add extra sugar to the final product. You can skip this step if you prefer, or experiment with different blanching times and methods to find your preferred result.

Kiwi slices: Slice the kiwis into thin slices, about **1/8 inch (3 mm)** thick. After preparing, spread the slices on the dehydrator trays in a single layer. Set the temperature to **135°F (57°C)** and dry for **6 to 10 hours**, depending on the humidity and the desired chewiness. Check for doneness by bending a slice; it should be flexible and not sticky. Kiwi slices are chewy and sweet, with a tangy kiwi flavor and aroma. You can enjoy them as a snack, use them as a topping for yogurt, cereal, or ice cream, or rehydrate them and use them as a filling for pies, cakes, or pastries.

Kiwi chips: Slice the kiwis into thick slices, about **1/4 inch (6 mm)** thick. Prepare it and sprinkle some honey, cinnamon, and nutmeg over the slices and toss to coat. Spread the slices on the dehydrator trays in a single layer. Set the temperature to **145°F (63°C)** and dry for **10 to 12 hours**, or until the slices are crisp and crunchy. Check for doneness by biting into a slice; it should not be chewy or moist. Kiwi chips are crispy and sweet, with a spicy kiwi flavor and aroma. You can enjoy them as a snack, or serve them with whipped cream, custard, or chocolate sauce.

Kiwi candy: Peel and dice the kiwis into small pieces, about **1/4 inch (6 mm)** in size. Transfer the pieces to a large pot and add enough water to cover them. Bring to a boil and then reduce the heat and simmer for 20 to 30 minutes, stirring occasionally, until the kiwis are soft and mushy. Mash the kiwis with a potato masher or a fork and add 2 cups (400 g) of sugar and 1/4 cup (60 ml) of lemon juice. Cook over medium-high heat, stirring constantly, until the mixture is thick and sticky. Drop the mixture by teaspoonfuls onto a baking mat lined with parchment paper and let it cool completely. Place the baking mat with candies on the dehydrator trays in a single layer. Set the temperature to **135°F (57°C)** and dry for **8 to 10 hours**, or until the candy is dry and chewy. Check for doneness by biting into a candy; it should be soft and sticky, but not wet. Kiwi candies are chewy and sweet, with a tangy kiwi flavor and aroma.

Lemons

How to choose

The best lemons for dehydration are fresh, ripe, and juicy. They should have a bright yellow color and a smooth skin. Avoid lemons that are green, wrinkled, bruised, or have soft spots.

You can use any variety of lemons, such as Lisbon, Meyer, or Eureka, depending on your preference and availability. Each variety has a slightly different flavor, acidity, and sweetness. Meyer's lemons are sweeter and less acidic than other types, while Eureka lemons are more sour and tart.

How to prepare

Wash the lemons thoroughly under running water, and scrub them with a brush or a sponge to remove any dirt or wax. You can also soak them in a solution of water and vinegar for 15 minutes to disinfect them and remove any residue. Cut the lemons into thin slices, depending on your preference. Try to make the slices as even and uniform as possible. Remove any seeds from the slices or wedges, as they can add bitterness to the final product. You can use a toothpick or a small knife to pry them out.

How to blanch

Blanching is an optional step for lemons. To blanch the lemons in water, bring a large pot of water to a boil, and add a pinch of salt and a splash of lemon juice. Add the lemon slices or wedges in batches, and boil them for about 30 seconds. Then, transfer them to a bowl of ice water, and drain them well.

Blanching can help prevent the lemons from browning or losing their flavor during dehydration. However, it can also make them softer and stickier, and add extra sugar to the final product. You can skip this step if you prefer, or experiment with different blanching times and methods to find your preferred result.

Lemon slices: Cut the lemons into thin slices, about **1/8 inch (3 mm)** thick. Prepare it and spread the slices on the dehydrator trays in a single layer. Set the temperature to **135°F (57°C)** and dry for **6 to 8 hours**, or until the slices are dry and brittle. Check for doneness by breaking a slice in half; it should snap easily and not feel moist. Lemon slices have a sour and zesty lemon flavor and aroma, with a slightly bitter aftertaste. They have a bright yellow color and a translucent appearance. You can use them to add flavor and decoration to drinks, desserts, salads, or seafood. You can also grind them into a powder and use it as a spice.

Lemon zest: Peel the lemons and cut the peel into thin strips, about **1/4 inch (6 mm)** wide. Scrape off any white pith from the peel, as it can make the zest bitter. Place the peel strips on the dehydrator trays and set the temperature to **95°F (35°C)**. Dry for **8 to 10 hours**, or until the peel is dry and brittle. Check for doneness by bending a strip; it should break easily and not feel moist. Lemon zest has a concentrated lemon flavor and aroma, with a slight sweetness. It has a dark yellow color and a hard texture. You can use it to add flavor and color to baked goods, sauces, marinades, teas, or cocktails. You can also grind it into a powder and use it as a spice.

Lemon candy: Cut the lemons into wedges, about **1 inch (25 mm)** thick at the base. Remove any seeds and blanch the wedges in boiling water for 5 minutes. Drain the wedges and transfer them to a large pot. Add enough water to cover them and bring them to a boil. Add 2 cups (400 g) of sugar and simmer for 30 minutes, stirring occasionally. Drain the wedges and place them on the dehydrator trays in a single layer. Set the temperature to **135°F (57°C)** and dry for **10 to 12 hours**, or until the wedges are dry and chewy. Check for doneness by biting into a wedge; it should be soft and sticky, but not wet. Lemon candy is sweet and sour, with a chewy and juicy texture.

Lettuce

How to choose

- Choose fresh and crisp lettuce that has no signs of wilting, browning, or rotting. Fresh lettuce will have a bright green color and a firm texture. You can use any variety of lettuce, such as romaine, iceberg, butterhead, or leaf lettuce.

How to prepare

- Wash the lettuce thoroughly and pat it dry with a clean towel or paper towel. Washing the lettuce will remove any dirt, insects, or pesticides that may be on the leaves.

- Remove any damaged or discolored leaves and discard them. Damaged leaves may have holes, tears, or spots that can affect the quality and taste of the dehydrated lettuce. Discolored leaves may have yellow, brown, or black areas that indicate decay or disease.

- Cut the lettuce into bite-sized pieces or leave them whole, depending on your preference. Cutting the lettuce will make it easier to fit on the dehydrator trays and reduce the dehydration time. Leaving the lettuce whole will preserve its shape and appearance.

How to blanch

- Blanching is not necessary for dehydrating lettuce, as it will retain its color and flavor without it. Blanching can also cause some nutrient loss and flavor change, and it adds an extra step to the dehydration process.

- However, if you want to blanch your lettuce, you can do so by boiling it for 30 seconds and then plunging it into ice water to stop the cooking process. This will deactivate the enzymes that can cause browning and spoilage, and it will also soften the lettuce slightly, making it easier to dehydrate. Drain the lettuce well and pat it dry before dehydrating it.

Lettuce flakes: Prepare it and tear it into small pieces, about **1 inch (25 mm)** in size. Spread the pieces on the dehydrator trays in a single layer. Set the temperature to **95°F (35°C)** and dry for **4 to 6 hours**, or until the pieces are dry and crisp. Check for doneness by crushing a piece with your fingers; it should crumble easily and not feel moist. Lettuce flakes have a mild and grassy lettuce flavor and aroma, with a crunchy texture. They have a light green color and a flaky shape. You can use them to add flavor and texture to soups, salads, sandwiches, or wraps. You can also rehydrate them by soaking them in water for about 10 minutes.

Lettuce wraps: Separate the leaves. Choose the large and sturdy ones for the wraps and save the small and tender ones for other uses. Prepare it and place the leaves on the dehydrator trays in a single layer. Set the temperature to **95°F (35°C)** and dry for **2 to 4 hours**, or until the leaves are dry and crisp. Check for doneness by breaking a leaf; it should snap easily and not feel moist. Lettuce wraps have a light and crunchy texture, with a mild and refreshing lettuce flavor and aroma. They have a light green color and a curved shape. You can use them to make low-carb and gluten-free wraps, by filling them with your choice of meat, cheese, vegetables, or sauces. You can also rehydrate them by dipping them in water for a few seconds and use them as fresh lettuce leaves.

Lettuce powder: Prepare it and cut it into thin strips, about **1/4 inch (6 mm)** wide. Spread the strips on the dehydrator trays in a single layer. Set the temperature to **95°F (35°C)** and dry for **6 to 8 hours,** or until the strips are dry and brittle. Check for doneness by breaking a strip with your fingers; it should snap easily and not feel sticky. Transfer the dried strips to a blender or a spice grinder and process them into a fine powder. Lettuce powder has a concentrated and fresh lettuce flavor and aroma, with a slight bitterness. It has a dark green color and a fine texture. You can use it to add flavor and color to smoothies, juices, dressings, dips, or sauces. You can also mix it with salt, pepper, garlic, and onion to make your lettuce seasoning.

Limes

How to choose

- The best limes for dehydrating are fresh, firm, and juicy. Avoid limes that are soft, wrinkled, or have brown spots.
- You can use any variety of limes, such as generic green limes, key limes, Tahiti limes, or kaffir limes. Each type has a slightly different flavor and size, so you may need to adjust the drying time accordingly.

How to prepare

- Wash the limes well, even if they are organic. You can soak them in a 50/50 solution of water and vinegar for about 15 minutes to remove any residue and wax on the skins. You can also scrub them with baking soda if you feel it necessary.
- Slice the limes into thin and even slices, about 1/4 inch thick or larger cubes, depending on your preference. A uniform thickness will ensure even drying.
- Remove any seeds or unwanted parts from the slices. You can leave the peel on, as it adds flavor and nutrients to the dried limes.

How to blanch

- Blanching is not necessary for dehydrating limes, as they have a high acidity that prevents browning and microbial growth.
- However, if you want to soften the peel and reduce the bitterness, you can blanch the lime slices in boiling water for a few seconds, then plunge them into ice water to stop the cooking process.

Lime slices: Cut the limes into thin slices, about **1/8 inch (3 mm)** thick. Prepare it and spread the slices on the dehydrator trays in a single layer. Set the temperature to **135°F (57°C)** and dry for **6 to 8 hours**, or until the slices are dry and brittle. Check for doneness by breaking a slice in half; it should snap easily and not feel moist. Lime slices have a sour and zesty lime flavor and aroma, with a slightly bitter aftertaste. They have a bright green color and a translucent appearance. You can use them to add flavor and decoration to drinks, desserts, salads, or seafood. You can also grind them into a powder and use it as a spice.

Lime zest: Peel the limes and cut the peel into thin strips, about **1/4 inch (6 mm)** wide. Scrape off any white pith from the peel, as it can make the zest bitter. Place the peel strips on the dehydrator trays and set the temperature to **95°F (35°C)**. Dry for **8 to 10 hours**, or until the peel is dry and brittle. Check for doneness by bending a strip; it should break easily and not feel moist. Lime zest has a concentrated lime flavor and aroma, with a slight sweetness. It has a dark green color and a hard texture. You can use it to add flavor and color to baked goods, sauces, marinades, teas, or cocktails. You can also grind it into a powder and use it as a spice.

Lime candy: Cut the limes into wedges, about **1 inch (25 mm)** thick at the base. Remove any seeds and blanch the wedges in boiling water for 5 minutes. Drain the wedges and transfer them to a large pot. Add enough water to cover them and bring them to a boil. Add 2 cups (400 g) of sugar and simmer for 30 minutes, stirring occasionally. Drain the wedges and place them on the dehydrator trays in a single layer. Set the temperature to **135°F (57°C)** and dry for **10 to 12 hours**, or until the wedges are dry and chewy. Check for doneness by biting into a wedge; it should be soft and sticky, but not wet. Lime candy is sweet and sour, with a chewy and juicy texture. It has a bright green color and a shiny surface. You can coat it with sugar or chocolate for extra sweetness, or enjoy it as it is. You can also use it as a decoration for cakes or cupcakes.

Mangoes

How to choose

The first step is to choose ripe and juicy mangoes that are free of bruises, blemishes, or soft spots. You can use any variety of mangoes, but some of the most popular ones for dehydrating are Alphonso, Kent, Keitt, and Tommy Atkins. You will need about 4 to 5 mangoes for one tray of dehydrated slices.

How to prepare

The next step is to wash, peel, and slice the mangoes. You can use a sharp knife or a peeler to remove the skin and then cut the flesh away from the large seed in the center. You can slice the mangoes into thin strips, wedges, or cubes, depending on your preference. The thinner the slices, the faster they will dry. Try to make the slices as uniform as possible, so they will dehydrate evenly.

How to blanch

Blanching is an optional step. To blanch the mangoes, you will need a large pot of water, a bowl of ice water, a slotted spoon, and a colander. Bring a large pot of water to a boil. You can add about 1/4 cup of sugar, 2 tablespoons of lemon juice, or 1 teaspoon of ascorbic acid per quart of water if desired. Add the mango slices to the boiling water in batches, and let them cook for about 30 seconds. Use a slotted spoon to transfer the mango slices to the bowl of ice water, and let them cool for a few minutes. Drain the mango slices in a colander, and pat them dry with paper towels.

Mango slices: Slice the mangoes into thin slices, about **1/8 inch (3 mm)** thick. Prepare it and spread the slices on the dehydrator trays in a single layer. Set the temperature to **135°F (57°C)** and dry for **6 to 10 hours**, depending on the humidity and the desired chewiness. Check for doneness by bending a slice; it should be flexible and not sticky. Mango slices are chewy and sweet, with a tropical mango flavor and aroma. They have a bright yellow-orange color and a flat shape. You can enjoy them as a snack, use them as a topping for yogurt, cereal, or ice cream, or rehydrate them and use them as a filling for pies, cakes, or pastries.

Mango chips: Slice the mangoes into thick slices, about **1/4 inch (6 mm)** thick. Prepare it and sprinkle some honey, cinnamon, and nutmeg over the slices and toss to coat. Spread the slices on the dehydrator trays in a single layer. Set the temperature to **145°F (63°C)** and dry for **10 to 12 hours**, or until the slices are crisp and crunchy. Check for doneness by biting into a slice; it should not be chewy or moist. Mango chips are crispy and sweet, with a spicy mango flavor and aroma. They have a golden brown color and a round shape. You can enjoy them as a snack, or serve them with whipped cream, custard, or chocolate sauce.

Mango candy: Peel and dice the mangoes into small pieces, about **1/4 inch (6 mm)** in size. Transfer the pieces to a large pot and add enough water to cover them. Bring to a boil and then reduce the heat and simmer for 20 to 30 minutes, stirring occasionally, until the mangoes are soft and mushy. Mash the mangoes with a potato masher or a fork, and add 2 cups (400 g) of sugar and 1/4 cup (60 ml) of lemon juice. Cook over medium-high heat, stirring constantly, until the mixture is thick and sticky. Drop the mixture by teaspoonfuls onto a baking mat lined with parchment paper and let it cool completely. Place the baking mat with candies on the dehydrator trays. Set the temperature to **135°F (57°C)** and dry for **8 to 10 hours**, or until the candy is dry and chewy. Check for doneness by biting into a candy; it should be soft and sticky, but not wet. Mango candy is chewy and sweet, with a tangy mango flavor and aroma. They have a bright yellow-orange color and a round shape. You can enjoy them as a treat, or use them as a decoration for cakes or cupcakes.

Mushrooms

How to choose

- The best mushrooms for dehydration are fresh, firm, and free of bruises, spots, or mold. These mushrooms will have the best flavor and texture after drying and will last longer in storage.

- You can use any variety of edible mushrooms, such as white button, shiitake, oyster, or chanterelle. Different mushrooms will have different tastes, textures, and colors when dehydrated, so you can experiment with different combinations and recipes.

- Avoid mushrooms that are slimy, wrinkled, or have a strong odor. These mushrooms are likely spoiled or contaminated and can cause food poisoning or allergic reactions. You should also avoid wild mushrooms that you are not sure about, as some of them can be poisonous or hallucinogenic.

- Small and medium-sized mushrooms with closed caps provide the best flavor and texture when rehydrated. Large mushrooms with deep gills like portabellos can result in a less-than-desirable dehydrated mushroom.

- Selecting fresh mushrooms with no bruises and blemishes ensures the highest quality of dehydrated mushrooms. You can also look for mushrooms that have a pleasant earthy smell.

How to prepare

- Wash the mushrooms gently under cold running water to remove any dirt or debris.
- Trim off any tough or woody stems.
- Cut the mushrooms into thin slices, about 1/4 inch thick, or leave them whole if they are small.
- If you want to prevent the mushrooms from browning, you can soak them in a solution of water and lemon juice (1/4 cup of lemon juice per quart of water) for about 10 minutes, then drain well.

How to blanch

- To blanch mushrooms, bring a large pot of water to a boil and add a pinch of salt.
- Add the mushrooms in batches and boil for about 5 minutes, or until they are tender.
- Drain the mushrooms and pat them dry with paper towels.

Mushroom slices: Prepare the mushrooms as above and cut them into thin slices, about **1/8 inch (3 mm)** thick. Spread the slices on the dehydrator trays in a single layer. Set the temperature to **125°F (52°C)** and dry for **4 to 6 hours**, or until the slices are dry and leathery. Check for doneness by bending a slice; it should not break easily and not feel moist. Mushroom slices have a mild and earthy mushroom flavor and aroma, with a slightly chewy texture. You can use them to add flavor and texture to soups, stews, casseroles, omelets, or pizzas. You can also rehydrate them by soaking them in water or broth for about 20 minutes. Another great idea is to make mushroom broths, add 1 tablespoon (8 g) of dried mushroom pieces to a cup of boiling water and steep for 10 to 15 minutes. The mushroom broth has a mild and soothing mushroom flavor and aroma, with a slight sweetness. It has a light brown color and a clear appearance. You can use it as a base for soups, broths, or risotto.

Mushroom jerky: This mushroom jerky recipe is the vegan version of beef jerky. Prepare the mushrooms and cut them into thin strips, about **1/4 inch (6 mm)** wide. In a large bowl, whisk together 1/4 cup (60 ml) of soy sauce, 2 tablespoons (30 ml) of maple syrup, 1 tablespoon (15 ml) of apple cider vinegar, 1 teaspoon (5 ml) of liquid smoke, 1/2 teaspoon (2.5 g) of smoked paprika, 1/4 teaspoon (1.25 g) of garlic powder, and 1/4 teaspoon (1.25 g) of black pepper. Add the mushroom strips and toss to coat. Cover the bowl and refrigerate for at least 4 hours or overnight to marinate. Drain the mushroom strips and place them on the dehydrator trays in a single layer. Set the temperature to **145°F (63°C)** and dry for **10 to 12 hours**, or until the mushroom strips are dry and chewy. Check for doneness by bending a strip; it should not break easily and not feel moist. Mushroom jerky is savory and smoky, with a chewy and meaty texture. It has a dark brown color and a flat shape. You can enjoy it as a snack, or use it as a protein source for hiking, camping, or traveling.

Okra

How to Choose
- The best okra for dehydrating are young, tender, and fresh pods that are about 2 to 4 inch long. Avoid pods that are too large, woody, or bruised, as they will not dehydrate well.
- You can use fresh or frozen okra for dehydrating, but fresh okra will have more flavor and texture. If you use frozen okra, thaw it completely and pat it dry before dehydrating.

How to Prepare
Wash the okra pods under cold running water and scrub them gently to remove any dirt or debris. Pat them dry with a clean towel or paper towel. Trim off the stem and tip ends of the okra pods with a sharp knife. You can also cut off any brown spots or blemishes on the pods. Cut the okra into your desired shape and size, and try to make the slices or halves as uniform as possible for even drying.

How to Blanch
- Blanching is an optional step that can help preserve the color, flavor, and texture of the okra.
- To blanch okra, bring a large pot of water to a boil and add some salt and vinegar. The salt will help season the okra and the vinegar will help prevent them from turning brown.
- Add the okra to the boiling water in batches and cook for about 2 minutes, or until they turn bright green. Do not overcook them, as they will become mushy and lose their shape.
- Drain the okra and immediately transfer them to a large bowl of ice water to cool them down and stop the cooking process. Drain them again and pat them dry with a towel or paper towel.
- Proceed with seasoning and dehydrating the okra as usual.

Okra chips or slices: Wash and trim the okra and cut them into thin slices, about **1/8 inch (3 mm)** thick for chips or **1/4 inch (6 mm)** for slices. Sprinkle some salt, pepper, and paprika over the slices and toss to coat. Spread the slices on the dehydrator trays in a single layer. Set the temperature to **135°F (57°C)** and dry for **6 to 8 hours**, slices will take longer to cook than chips there is no exact cooking time, just cook until the slices are crisp and crunchy. Check for doneness by biting into a slice; it should not be chewy or moist. Okra chips are crispy and savory, with a mild okra flavor and a hint of spice. They have a green color and a round shape. You can enjoy them as a snack, or serve them with dips, salsa, or cheese.

Okra powder: Wash and trim the okra and cut them into small pieces, about **1/4 inch (6 mm)** in size. Spread the pieces on the dehydrator trays in a single layer. Set the temperature to **135°F (57°C)** and dry for **8 to 10 hours**, or until the pieces are completely dry and hard. Check for doneness by crushing a piece with your fingers; it should crumble easily and not feel sticky. Transfer the dried pieces to a blender or a spice grinder and process them into a fine powder. Okra powder has a subtle and earthy okra flavor and aroma, with a slight sweetness. It has a light green color and a fine texture. You can use it to add flavor and thickness to soups, stews, curries, or sauces. You can also mix it with water and drink it as a health tonic.

Okra jerky: Prepare and cut them into thin strips, about **1/4 inch (6 mm)** wide. In a large bowl, whisk together 1/4 cup (60 ml) of soy sauce, 2 tablespoons (30 ml) of Worcestershire sauce, 1 tablespoon (15 ml) of honey, 1 teaspoon (5 ml) of liquid smoke, 1/2 teaspoon (2.5 g) of garlic powder, 1/4 teaspoon (1.25 g) of onion powder, 1/4 teaspoon (1.25 g) of black pepper, and 1/8 teaspoon (0.625 g) of cayenne pepper. Add the okra strips and toss to coat. Cover the bowl and refrigerate for at least 4 hours or overnight to marinate. Drain the okra and place them on the dehydrator trays in a single layer. Set the temperature to **145°F (63°C)** and dry for **8 to 10 hours**, or until the okra are dry and chewy. Check for doneness by bending a strip; it should not break easily and not feel moist. Okra jerky is savory and smoky, with a chewy and meaty texture. It has a dark brown color and a flat shape. You can enjoy it as a snack, or use it as a protein source for hiking, camping, or traveling.

Onions

How to choose

- Choose fresh, firm, and dry onions with no signs of sprouting or decay. Yellow, white, or red onions can be used, depending on your preference and recipe.
- Avoid using sweet onions, such as Vidalia or Walla Walla, as they have a higher water content and may not dehydrate well.

How to prepare

- Peel and wash the onions under cold running water. Pat them dry with a paper towel or a clean cloth. Cut the onions into the slices, you prefer.
- Blanching is optional for dehydrating onions, but it may help reduce the strong odor and taste of raw onions. To blanch onions, bring a large pot of water to a boil and add a pinch

of salt. Add the onion slices and boil for about 30 seconds, then drain and rinse them under cold water to stop the cooking process. Alternatively, you can steam the onion slices for about 2 minutes over boiling water, then cool them under cold water. After blanching, pat the onion slices dry with a paper towel or a clean cloth before placing them on dehydrator trays.

Onion flakes: Peel and chop the onions into small pieces, about **1/4 inch (6 mm)** in size. Spread the pieces on the dehydrator trays in a single layer. Set the temperature to **145°F (63°C)** and dry for **4 to 6 hours**, or until the pieces are dry and crisp. Check for doneness by crushing a piece with your fingers; it should crumble easily and not feel moist. Onion flakes have a strong and pungent onion flavor and aroma, with a slightly sweet aftertaste. They have a light brown color and a flaky texture. You can use them to add flavor to soups, stews, casseroles, dips, or salads. You can also rehydrate them by soaking them in water for about 15 minutes.

Onion powder: Peel and slice the onions into thin rings, about **1/8 inch (3 mm)** thick. Separate the rings and spread them on the dehydrator trays in a single layer. Set the temperature to **145°F (63°C)** and dry for **6 to 8 hours**, or until the rings are dry and brittle. Check for doneness by breaking a ring with your fingers; it should snap easily and not feel sticky. Transfer the dried rings to a blender or a spice grinder and process them into a fine powder. Onion powder has a concentrated and sharp onion flavor and scent, with a slight bitterness. It has a dark brown color and a fine texture. You can use it to add flavor and color to sauces, marinades, rubs, dressings, or popcorn. You can also mix it with other spices to make your seasoning blend.

Onion rings: Peel and slice the onions into thick rings, about **1/2 inch (12 mm)** thick. Separate the rings and dip them in a batter made of 1 cup (125 g) of all-purpose flour, 1 teaspoon (5 g) of baking powder, 1/2 teaspoon (2.5 g) of salt, 1/4 teaspoon (1.25 g) of black pepper, and 1 cup (240 ml) of water. Shake off any excess batter and place the rings on the dehydrator trays in a single layer. Set the temperature to **145°F (63°C)** and dry for **8 to 10 hours**, or until the rings are dry and crunchy. Check for doneness by biting into a ring; it should be crisp and not chewy. Onion rings are crispy and savory, with a soft and tender onion inside. They have a golden brown color and a round shape. You can enjoy them as a snack, or serve them with ketchup, mustard, or barbecue sauce.

Some tips and tricks

- To prevent tears while cutting onions, you can chill them in the refrigerator for about 30 minutes before slicing, or wear goggles or glasses to protect your eyes.
- To reduce the strong smell of onions in your kitchen, you can dehydrate them outdoors, in a well-ventilated area, or near an open window or a fan.
- To prevent the onion flavor from transferring to other foods in your dehydrator, you can dehydrate onions separately, or use separate trays and screens for different foods.

Oranges

How to choose

The best oranges for dehydration are fresh, ripe, and juicy. Avoid oranges that are bruised, moldy, or dry. You can use any variety of oranges, such as navel, Valencia, blood, or mandarin. However, some types may have thicker skins, more seeds, or less juice than others, so you may need to adjust your drying time accordingly.

How to prepare

To prepare oranges for dehydration, you need to wash them well and dry them with a clean towel. Then, cut off the ends and slice them thinly, about 1/4 inch thick or less. You can use a sharp knife or a mandolin slicer for this. Try to make the slices as uniform as possible, so they dry evenly. Remove any seeds or white pith from the slices, as they can make the oranges bitter.

How to blanch

To blanch oranges, bring a large pot of water to a boil and add some lemon juice or citric acid to prevent oxidation. Then, add the orange slices and boil them for about 30 seconds. Drain them and plunge them into ice water to stop the cooking process. Pat them dry with paper towels before placing them on the dehydrator trays.

Orange chips: Cut the oranges into thin slices, about **1/8 inch (3 mm)** thick. Prepare it and spread the slices on the dehydrator trays in a single layer. Set the temperature to **135°F (57°C)** and dry for **6 to 12 hours**, depending on the humidity and the desired crispiness. Check for doneness by breaking a slice in half; it should be brittle and snap easily. Orange chips are crunchy and sweet, with a tangy citrus flavor. They have a bright orange color and a translucent appearance. You can enjoy them as a snack, use them as a garnish, or dip them in chocolate for a decadent treat.

Orange candy: Cut the oranges into wedges, about **1 inch (25 mm)** thick at the base. Prepare and blanch the wedges in boiling water for 5 minutes. Drain the wedges and transfer them to a large pot. Add enough water to cover them and bring them to a boil. Add 2 cups (400 g) of sugar and simmer for 30 minutes, stirring occasionally. Drain the wedges and place them on the dehydrator trays. Set the temperature to **135°F (57°C)** and dry for **10 to 12 hours**, or until the wedges are dry and chewy. Check for doneness by biting into a wedge; it should be soft and sticky, but not wet. Orange candy is sweet and sour, with a chewy and juicy texture. It has a dark orange color and a shiny surface. You can coat it with sugar or chocolate for extra sweetness, or enjoy it as it is. You can also use it as a decoration for cakes or cupcakes.

Papaya

How to choose

When selecting papaya, it is important to choose a ripe fruit. Ripe papaya should be mostly yellow with some green areas, and it should feel slightly soft to the touch. Avoid papayas that are completely green or have blemishes or bruises.

How to prepare

Before preparing papaya for dehydration, it should be washed thoroughly. Use a vegetable brush to gently scrub the skin and remove any dirt or debris. Once washed, the papaya should be dried with a clean towel. Then, cut the papaya in half lengthwise and remove the seeds using a spoon. Peel the papaya and then slice it into the slices you prefer.

How to blanch

Blanching is not required for dehydrating papaya, but it can help retain the color and flavor of the fruit. If you know you will be using the papaya with gelatin or in baking, you can steam it over boiling water for 1 to 2 minutes. Otherwise, you can lightly spray the papaya slices with lemon juice or an ascorbic acid solution to prevent discoloration.

Papaya chips: These are thin slices of papaya that are dried until crisp and crunchy. To make them, you will need to slice the papaya into **1/8 inch (3 mm)** thick slices and soak them in a lemon juice solution to prevent browning. Then, place them on a dehydrator tray and dry at **125°F (52°C)** for about **10 hours**, or until they snap when bent. You can check for doneness by breaking a piece and looking for any moisture inside. One pound (454 g) of raw papaya will yield about **2 ounces (57 g)** of dried chips. Papaya chips are sweet and tangy, with a bright orange color and a smooth texture. They are great for snacking, adding to trail mix, or topping yogurt or cereal.

Papaya chunks: These are bite-sized pieces of papaya that are dried until chewy and tender. To make them, you will need to cut the papaya into **1/2 inch (12 mm)** cubes and dry them at **125°F (52°C)** for **about 14 hours**, or until they are soft and pliable. You can check for doneness by squeezing a piece and feeling for any moisture. One pound (454 g) of raw papaya will yield about **3 ounces (85 g)** of dried chunks. Papaya chunks are juicy and succulent, with a bright yellow color and a smooth texture. They are delicious as a snack, or as an addition to salads, granola, or oatmeal.

Papaya flakes: These are thin and crisp flakes of papaya that are dried until they shatter when crushed. To make them, you will need to peel and grate the papaya using a box grater or a food processor. Then, spread the grated papaya on a dehydrator tray and dry at **125°F (52°C)** for about **6 hours**, or until they are dry and brittle. You can check for doneness by crumbling a flake and looking for any moisture. One pound (454 g) of raw papaya will yield about **1 ounce (28 g)** of dried flakes. Papaya flakes are light and crunchy, with a pale orange color and a subtle sweetness. They can be used to garnish desserts, ice cream, or cocktails, or to add some texture and flavor to soups, stews, or curries.

Peaches

How to choose

The best peaches for dehydrating are ripe, firm, and sweet. Avoid peaches that are overripe, bruised, or moldy. You can use either freestone or clingstone peaches, but freestone peaches are easier to pit and slice. You can also use fresh, frozen, or canned peaches, but fresh peaches will have the best flavor and texture.

How to prepare

Before dehydrating, you need to wash, peel, pit, and slice the peaches. To wash the peaches, rinse them under cold water and gently rub the skin to remove any dirt or insects. To peel the peaches, you can either use a knife or a peeler, or you can blanch them first to make the skin come off easily. To pit the peaches, cut them in half vertically and twist the halves apart. If you are using freestone peaches, the pit should come out easily. If you are using clingstone peaches, you may need to use a knife to cut the flesh away from the pit. To slice the peaches, cut them into thin and even slices, about 1/8 to 1/4 inch thick. Thicker slices will take longer to dry and maybe chewier. Thinner slices may stick to the dehydrator trays and tear. To prevent the peaches from browning, you can soak them in a solution of water and lemon juice or vinegar for a few minutes. This step is optional, but it will help preserve the color and flavor of the peaches.

How to blanch

To blanch the peaches, you need a large pot of boiling water, a large bowl of ice water, a slotted spoon, and a knife. Here are the steps to blanch the peaches:

Bring a large pot of water to a boil over high heat. Use a knife to score a small "x" on the bottom of each peach. This will help the skin peel off easily. Put the peaches into the boiling water for about one minute. Do not overcrowd the pot, and work in batches if needed. Remove the peaches from the boiling water with a slotted spoon and transfer them to the ice water. Let them soak in the cold water for a few minutes, until they are cool enough to handle. Peel the peaches by hand, using the knife to help with any stubborn spots. The skin should come off easily, but be careful not to bruise or damage the flesh.

Peach halves: These are whole peach halves that are dried until they are leathery and firm. Halve the peaches after preparation. Then, place them on the dehydrator trays, and cut side up. Set the dehydrator temperature to **135°F (57°C)** and dry the peaches for **18 to 24 hours**, rotating the trays and checking the peaches every few hours. You can tell they are done when they are dry to the touch and no moisture beads form when you squeeze them. One pound of fresh peaches will yield about **3 ounces (85 g)** of dried peach halves. You can use them as a snack, in compotes, jams, pies, cobblers, chutneys, and more. They have a deep orange color, a rich and concentrated flavor, and a chewy and dense texture.

Peach chips or slices: These are thin and crispy slices of peaches that are great for snacking or adding to granola. To make them, you need to slice the peaches into **1/8 inch (3 mm)** slices for chips and **1/4 inch (6 mm)** for slices. Place them on the dehydrator trays in a single layer. Dehydrate at **135°F (57°C)** for **10 to 12 hours**, or until they are dry and crisp. You can peel the peaches before slicing them, or leave the skin on for extra fiber and flavor. 1 pound (454 g) of fresh peaches will yield about **2 ounces (57 g)** of peach chips. To check for doneness, break a chip in half and look for any signs of moisture. If the chip is still pliable, it needs more drying time. Peach chips have a sweet and tangy taste and a light orange color. They are crunchy and brittle.

Pears

How to Choose

- The best variety of pears for dehydrating is Bartlett, which has a smooth texture and a rich flavor. Other varieties, such as Anjou, Bosc, or Comice, can also be used, but they may have a grittier texture or a milder taste.
- Choose pears that are ripe but not too soft. They should have a yellow or green color, depending on the variety, and a slight give when pressed gently. Avoid pears that are bruised, damaged, or overripe, as they will not dehydrate well.
- You can use fresh or frozen pears for dehydrating. If using frozen peas, thaw them completely before peeling and slicing them.

How to Prepare

Wash the pears with soap and water to remove any dirt, wax, or pesticides. You can use a scrub brush to clean them thoroughly. Peel the pears with a vegetable peeler or a knife. Most of the gritty texture of pears comes from the cells just under the skin, so peeling them will result in a smoother product. Cut the pears into quarters and remove the cores and stems. You can use a knife, a pear corer, or a loop tool to do this. Slice the pears into slices if you prefer. Drop the pear slices into a large bowl of water with lemon juice or vinegar. This will prevent them from browning while they dry. Use about 1 tablespoon of lemon juice or vinegar per quart of water.

How to blanch

Blanching is an optional step that can help preserve the color, flavor, and texture of the pears. To blanch pears in water, bring a large pot of water to a boil and add the pear slices. Boil them for about 2 minutes, then drain and rinse them with cold water. Pat them dry with a paper towel before placing them on the dehydrator trays. To blanch pears in syrup, make a simple syrup by combining 2 cups of sugar and 4 cups of water in a saucepan. Bring it to a boil and add the pear slices. Simmer them for about 10 minutes, then drain and cool them. Pat them dry with a paper towel before placing them on the dehydrator trays. You can also add spices, such as cinnamon, nutmeg, ginger, or cardamom, to the water or syrup for extra flavor.

Pear chips: These are thin and crispy slices of pears that are great for snacking or adding to granola, oatmeal, or yogurt. To make pear chips, slice prepared fruits thinly with a mandolin or a knife about **1/8 inch (3mm)** thick. Arrange them in a single layer on the dehydrator trays. Sprinkle with cinnamon and honey if desired. Dehydrate at **135°F (57°C)** for **6 to 18 hours**, or until crisp and dry. Check for doneness by breaking a slice in half; there should be no moisture beads. Store in an airtight container for up to a year. Pear chips have a sweet and fruity flavor, a golden-brown color, and a crunchy texture.

Pear chunks: These are bite-sized pieces of pears that are ideal for adding to trail mix, cereal, muffins, or cookies. To make pear chunks, dice the pears, and spread them on the dehydrator trays so that the fruits do not touch each other. Dehydrate at **135°F (57°C)** for **10 to 12 hours**, or until dry and chewy. Check for doneness by squeezing a chunk; it should be firm but not hard. Store in an airtight container for up to a year. Pear chunks have a sweet and mild flavor, a light-yellow color, and a chewy and spongy texture.

Peas

How to choose

Opt for fresh peas that are bright green, plump, and firm. They should feel heavy for their size, indicating a good amount of moisture and freshness. If you're using garden peas, ensure the pods are smooth and unblemished. For sugar snap or snow peas, the pods should be crisp and snap easily when bent. Avoid peas that are yellowing, wrinkled, or have spots, as these are signs of age and may not dehydrate as well.

How to prepare

Rinse the peas under cold water to remove any dirt or debris. If using garden peas, shell them to release the individual peas. For sugar snap and snow peas, trim the ends and remove any tough strings along the sides of the pods. If you prefer, you can split the pods open to check for and remove any pests or imperfections before dehydrating.

How to blanch

Blanching is a crucial step for dehydrating peas as it helps to preserve their color, flavor, and nutritional content. Bring a large pot of water to a rolling boil. Add the peas and blanch for 1.5 to 2.5 minutes, depending on their size. Immediately after blanching, transfer the peas to a bowl of ice water to stop the cooking process and lock in their vibrant green color. Drain the peas thoroughly and pat them dry with a clean kitchen towel or paper towel to remove excess moisture.

Whole peas: These are the simplest and most common way to dehydrate peas. You can use fresh, frozen, or canned peas, but frozen peas are the easiest as they don't require any pre-treatment. To dehydrate whole peas, simply spread them out on a dehydrator tray lined with a mesh sheet or parchment paper. Set the dehydrator to **125°F (52°C)** and dry them for **6 to 10 hours** until they are hard and brittle[12]. To check for doneness, let them cool and then try to squeeze one between your fingers. It should not be soft or squishy at all[2]. 1 pound of raw peas will yield about **3 ounces (85 grams)** of dried peas. Whole dried peas have a bright green color and a sweet and nutty flavor. They can be rehydrated by soaking them in hot water for 15 minutes or adding them to soups, stews, casseroles, or other dishes that use a lot of liquid.

Pea flakes: These are peas that have been flattened into thin flakes. They are similar to oat flakes or rolled oats and have a light and crispy texture. Pea flakes are often used to make porridge, granola, or baked goods, such as cookies, muffins, or bread. To dehydrate pea flakes, you can flake them yourself by soaking whole or split peas in water for 24 hours and then rolling them with a rolling pin or a pasta machine. Then, spread them out on a dehydrator tray lined with a mesh sheet or parchment paper. Set the dehydrator to **125°F (52°C)** and dry them for **4 to 6 hours** until they are dry and crisp. To check for doneness, let them cool and then try to snap one. It should not be soft or bendy at all. 1 pound of raw peas will yield about **5 ounces (142 grams)** of dried pea flakes. Dried pea flakes have a light green color and a flaky and crunchy texture. They can be cooked by simmering them in water or milk for 10 to 15 minutes or adding them to granola, cookies, muffins, or bread.

Pineapples

How to choose

The first step is to choose a ripe and fresh pineapple. You can tell if a pineapple is ripe by its color, smell, and feel. A ripe pineapple should have a golden-yellow skin, a sweet and fruity aroma, and a firm but slightly soft flesh. Avoid pineapples that are green, bruised, moldy, or have a sour or fermented smell.

How to prepare

Wash the pineapple under running water and pat it dry with a paper towel. Cut off the top and bottom of the pineapple and discard them.

Peel the pineapple by cutting off the skin in thin strips from top to bottom. Make sure to remove all the brown eyes and any remaining bits of skin. Cut the pineapple in half and remove the core by cutting a V-shaped wedge along the center of each half. Cut the pineapple into thin slices you prefer.

How to blanch

To blanch the pineapple, fill the pot with enough water or syrup to cover the pineapple slices. You can make your syrup by mixing 2 cups of sugar and 4 cups of water in a saucepan and bringing it to a boil. Bring the water or syrup to a boil over high heat. Add the pineapple slices to the boiling water or syrup and cook for about 2 minutes. Drain the pineapple slices and transfer them to a baking sheet lined with paper towels. Pat them dry with more paper towels.

Pineapple rings: Cut the pineapple into thin rings, about **1/4 inch (0.6 cm)** thick, and remove the core. Dehydrate at **135°F (57°C)** for **8 to 10 hours**, or until pliable and chewy. You can expect to get about **1/4 pound (113 g)** of dried pineapple rings from 1 pound (454 g) of fresh pineapple. To check for doneness, bend a ring and see if it breaks or cracks. If it does, it is over-dried and may be brittle. If it is soft and flexible, it is done. Pineapple rings are sweet and tangy, with a bright yellow color and a slightly sticky texture. They are great for snacking on their own or adding to trail mix, granola, oatmeal, or baked goods.

Pineapple chunks: Cut the pineapple into small chunks, about **1/2 inch (1.3 cm)** in size. Dehydrate at **135°F (57°C)** for **10 to 12 hours**, or until dry and crisp. You can expect to get about **1/5 pound (90 g)** of dried pineapple chunks from 1 pound (454 g) of fresh pineapple. To check for doneness, bite into a chunk and see if it is crunchy and brittle. If it is soft or moist, it needs more drying time. Pineapple chunks are crunchy and sweet, with a golden color and a hard texture. They are perfect for adding to cereal, yogurt, smoothies, or salads. You can also rehydrate them by soaking them in water or juice for a few hours.

Pineapple chips: Peel and core the pineapple, and slice it into thin rounds, about **1/8 inch (0.3 cm)** thick. Cut each round into quarters, and place them on the dehydrator trays in a single layer. Dehydrate at **135°F (57°C)** for **6 to 8 hours**, or until crisp and dry. You can expect to get about **1/6 pound (75 g)** of dried pineapple chips from 1 pound (454 g) of fresh pineapple. To check for doneness, snap a chip and see if it breaks easily. If it bends or tears, it is not dry enough. Pineapple chips are crispy and tart, with a light yellow color and a thin texture. They are delicious as a snack, or as a garnish for desserts, drinks, or ice cream. You can also dip them in chocolate or yogurt for a decadent treat.

Candied pineapple: Cut the pineapple into small pieces, about **1/2 inch (1.3 cm)** in size. Bring some water and sugar to a boil in a saucepan, and add the pineapple pieces. Simmer for about 15 minutes, or until the pineapple is soft and translucent. Drain the pineapple, and spread it on the dehydrator trays in a single layer. Dehydrate at **135°F (57°C)** for **12 to 14 hours**, or until dry and sticky. You can expect to get about **1/10 pound (45 g)** of candied pineapple from 1 pound (454 g) of fresh pineapple. To check for doneness, touch a piece and see if it is tacky and firm. If it is soft or moist, it needs more drying time. Candied pineapple is sweet and chewy, with a dark yellow color and a sticky texture. It is a festive and indulgent snack, or a wonderful addition to cakes, cookies, or breads. You can also coat it with sugar or coconut for extra sweetness and crunch.

Potatoes

How to choose

The best potatoes for dehydrating are ones that are firm, fresh, and free of bruises, sprouts, or green spots. You can use any variety of potatoes, but some may have different textures or flavors after dehydrating. For example, russet potatoes are starchy and fluffy, while red potatoes are waxy and creamy. You may want to experiment with different types of potatoes to find your preference.

How to prepare

Before dehydrating, you need to wash, peel, and slice your potatoes. You can use a knife, a mandolin, or a food processor to cut your potatoes into thin and even slices. The thinner the slices, the faster they will dehydrate. You can also cut your potatoes into cubes, shreds, or wedges, depending on how you want to use them later.

How to blanch

To blanch your potatoes, you need to bring a large pot of water to a boil and add some salt and lemon juice or vinegar. Then, add your potato slices and cook them for 3 to 5 minutes, depending on their thickness. After that, drain your potatoes and rinse them under cold water to stop the cooking process. You can also use a steam basket or a microwave to blanch your potatoes.

Potato chips: Cut the potatoes into thin slices about **1/16 inch (0.16 cm)** thick. Rinse them in cold water, then dry them with paper towels. Place the slices on a dehydrator tray in a single layer, sprinkle with salt to taste, and dehydrate at **125 °F (52 °C)** for **6-8 hours**, turning them once an hour. The chips should be crisp and slightly curled at the edges. From 1 pound (0.45 kg) of raw potatoes, you can get about **4 ounces (113 g)** of dehydrated chips. Dehydrated potato chips have a golden-brown color and a crunchy texture. They have a salty flavor, which you can change using different seasonings. You can eat them as a snack or add them to salads, soups, or sandwiches.

Potato chips (mashed potato): Prepare the mashed potato by adding some oil, salt, and any seasonings you like. You can use leftover mashed potato or make it from scratch. Spread the mashed potato evenly on a baking sheet lined with parchment paper. You can use a spatula or a piping bag to create thin and uniform layers. Dehydrate the potato at **125°F (52°C)** for **8-10 hours**, or until they are crispy and fully dehydrated. 1 pound (0.454 kg) of mashed potato, you will end up with about **4 ounces (113.4 g)** of potato chips. However, this may vary depending on the thickness and moisture of your mashed potatoes and how long you dehydrate them.

Potato cubes: Cut the potatoes into cubes about **1/4 inch (0.64 cm)** in size. Place them on a dehydrator tray in a single layer and dehydrate at **130 °F (54 °C)** for **10-12 hours**, turning them once every two hours. From 1 pound (0.45 kg) of raw potatoes, you can get about **3 ounces (85 g)** of dehydrated cubes. Dehydrated potato cubes have a light-yellow color and a hard or chewy texture, depending on how you decide to dry them. They have a neutral flavor, which you can enhance by adding salt, pepper, garlic, or other spices. You can use them to make potato soup, pie, casserole, or other dishes.

Potato mash: Cut the potatoes into thin slices about **1/8 inch (0.32 cm)** thick. Rinse them in cold water, then dry them with paper towels. Place the slices on a dehydrator tray in a single layer and dehydrate at **135 °F (57 °C)** for **8-10 hours**, turning them once every two hours. The slices should be brittle and moisture-free. Turn them into powder using a blender or a coffee grinder. Store the mash in an airtight container. From 1 pound (0.45 kg) of raw potatoes, you can get about **2 ounces (57 g)** of dehydrated mash. Dehydrated potato mash has a white color and a powdery texture. It has a soft flavor, which you can enrich by adding milk, butter, cheese, or other ingredients. You can use it to make mashed potatoes, croquettes, dumplings, or other desserts.

Plums/Prunes

How to choose

The first step to making dried plums is to choose the right variety and quality of plums. You can use any type of plum, but some varieties are better suited for drying than others. Freestone plums, such as Stanley and Damson, have pits that are easy to remove from the flesh, which makes them ideal for halving and drying. Clingstone plums, such as Santa Rosa and Satsuma, have pits that are firmly attached to the flesh, which makes them more difficult to halve and dry. You can either slice around the pits or dry them whole, but you will need to break the skins first to prevent casehardening.

You should also look for plums that are ripe, firm, and free of bruises, blemishes, and mold. Avoid plums that are overripe, soft, or wrinkled, as they will not dry well and may spoil. You can use slightly underripe plums, but they will have less flavor and sweetness than ripe ones.

How to prepare

Once you have chosen your plums, you need to wash them well and remove the stems and pits. If you are using freestone plums, you can simply cut them in half and twist them to separate the flesh from the pit. If you are using clingstone plums, you can either cut around the pit or discard it. You can also cut the plums into smaller pieces, such as quarters or slices if you prefer. Smaller pieces will dry faster and more evenly, but they will also shrink more and lose more flavor and nutrients.

How to blanch

Blanching can also help break the skins of whole plums, which allows the moisture to escape and prevents casehardening. To blanch plums in water, bring a large pot of water to a boil and add a small amount of lemon juice or citric acid to prevent browning. Add the plums in batches and boil for 30 seconds to 1 minute, depending on the size and ripeness of the plums. Remove the plums with a slotted spoon and transfer them to a bowl of ice water to cool. Drain the plums and pat them dry with paper towels.

To blanch plums in syrup, make a simple syrup by combining equal parts of sugar and water in a saucepan and bringing it to a boil. You can also add spices, such as cinnamon, cloves, or vanilla, for extra flavor. Add the plums in batches and simmer for 5 to 10 minutes, until the plums are soft but not mushy. Remove the plums with a slotted spoon and transfer them to a bowl of ice water to cool. Drain the plums and pat them dry with paper towels. You can reserve the syrup for another use, such as making jam or drizzling over desserts.

Prune chips: Cut the prunes into thin slices, about **1/8 inch (0.3 cm)** thick. Dehydrate at **135°F (57°C)** for **10 to 12 hours**, or until crisp and brittle. One pound (0.45 kg) of raw prunes will yield about **4 ounces (113 g)** of prune chips. To check for doneness, break a slice in half and look for any moisture beads. Prune chips are sweet and tangy, with a dark purple color and a crunchy texture. They are great for snacking, adding to granola, or topping yogurt or ice cream.

Prune powder: Cut the prunes into small pieces, about **1/4 inch (0.6 cm)** or smaller. Dehydrate at **135°F (57°C)** for **10 to 14 hours**, or until very dry and hard. One pound (0.45 kg) of raw prunes will yield about **6 ounces (170 g)** of prune powder. To check for doneness, grind a piece in a blender or spice grinder and look for any moisture clumps. Prune powder is sweet and fruity, with a dark purple color and a fine texture. It can be stored in an airtight jar or container. Prune powder can be used as a natural sweetener, a flavor enhancer, or a thickener for sauces, soups, or stews.

Prune nuggets: Cut the prunes into bite-sized slices, about **1/2 inch (1.3 cm)** or halves. Dehydrate at **140°F (60°C) for 6-10 hours (for slices) 24-36 hours (for halves)**, or until chewy and slightly sticky. One pound (0.45 kg) of raw prunes will yield about **8 ounces (226 g)** of prune nuggets. To check for doneness, squeeze a piece and look for any juice. Prune nuggets are sweet and sticky, with a dark purple color and a soft texture. They can be stored in an airtight bag or container, or coated with sugar, cocoa, or nuts to prevent them from sticking together. Prune nuggets are a tasty and convenient snack, or a fun addition to trail mix, cereal, or oatmeal.

Pumpkin

How to Choose

The best pumpkins for dehydration are the ones that have a rich orange color, a firm texture, and a sweet flavor. You can use any variety of pumpkins, but some of the most popular ones are sugar pumpkins, Long Island cheese pumpkins, and warty pumpkins. Avoid ornamental gourds, which may not be edible. You can also use other winter squashes, such as butternut squash, which has a similar taste and texture to pumpkin.

How to Prepare

To prepare pumpkin for dehydration, you need to wash it, cut it, and remove the seeds and pulp. You can save the seeds for roasting later, and you can also dehydrate the skins and pulp to make pumpkin powder. You can cut the pumpkin into slices, cubes, or chunks, depending on your preference and the size of your dehydrator trays. Furthermore, you can also puree the pumpkin and spread it on dehydrator sheets or baking paper to make pumpkin leather.

How to blanch

Blanching is optional for dehydrating pumpkins, but it can help prevent browning and improve the quality of the dried product. To blanch pumpkin, you can either steam it for 3 minutes or boil it for 2 minutes in water with a pinch of salt and lemon juice. After blanching, you need to drain the pumpkin and pat it dry with a paper towel before placing it on the dehydrator trays.

Pumpkin chips: Cut the raw pumpkin into thin slices, about **1/8 inch (3 mm)** thick. Place them on dehydrator trays in a single layer. Sprinkle some salt, honey, cinnamon, or other spices if desired. Dehydrate at **135°F (57°C)** for **6 to 8 hours**, or until crisp and brittle. One pound (454 g) of raw pumpkin will yield about **1 oz (28 g)** of dried chips. Pumpkin chips are crunchy and sweet, with a bright orange color. They make a great snack or garnish for salads and soups.

Pumpkin cubes: Peel and dice the raw pumpkin into small cubes, about **1/2 inch (13 mm)** or **1/4 inch (0.64 cm)** in size. Blanch the cubes in boiling water for 2 minutes, then drain and cool. Place the cubes on dehydrator trays in a single layer. Dehydrate at **135°F (57°C)** for **6 to 10 hours**, or until dry and hard. Pumpkin cubes shrink a lot when they are dry. 1 pound (454 g) of raw pumpkin will yield about **1 oz (28 g)** of dried cubes. Pumpkin cubes are firm and starchy, with a pale orange color. They can be rehydrated and used for stews, casseroles, or curries.

Pumpkin seeds: Scoop out the seeds from the pumpkin and rinse them well. Remove any pulp or strings. Soak the seeds in salted water for 8 hours, then drain and pat dry. Season the seeds with oil, salt, pepper, garlic, or other spices if desired. Place the seeds on dehydrator trays in a single layer. Dehydrate at **115°F (46°C)** for **12 to 24 hours** or until crisp and crunchy. One pound (454 g) of pumpkin will yield about **4 ounces (113 g)** of dried seeds. Pumpkin seeds are nutty and savory, with a greenish-white color. They are rich in protein, fiber, and minerals. They can be eaten as a snack, or added to salads, granola, or bread.

Radishes

How to choose

- Look for radishes that are firm, smooth, and brightly colored. Avoid radishes that are soft, wrinkled, or blemished.
- Choose radishes that are small to medium, as they tend to be milder and crisper than larger ones.
- If possible, buy radishes with their greens attached, as they indicate freshness and can also be dehydrated for a nutritious and flavorful garnish.

How to prepare

- Wash the radishes and their greens thoroughly under running water to remove any dirt or debris.
- Trim off the root ends and the leafy stems of the radishes, leaving about an inch of the greens attached.
- Rinse the radishes and pat them dry with a paper towel.

How to blanch

- To blanch your radishes, you will need a large pot of water, a large bowl of ice water, a slotted spoon, and a colander.
- Bring the pot of water to a boil and add a pinch of salt.
- Add the radish slices and greens to the boiling water and cook for about 30 seconds, or until they are slightly tender but still crisp.
- Use the slotted spoon to transfer the radishes and greens to the ice water and let them cool completely.
- Drain the radishes and greens in the colander and pat them dry with a paper towel.

Radish coins or cubes: Slice the radishes into **1/4 inch (0.6 cm)** thick coins or cubes. Prepare and toss them with some olive oil, salt, and pepper, and spread them in a single layer on the dehydrator trays. Dehydrate at **125°F (52°C)** for **4 to 6 hours**, or until crisp and dry. 1 pound (0.45 kg) of fresh radishes will yield about **1.5oz (42g)** of dried radish coins. They have a mild spicy flavor, a light pink color, and a crunchy texture. They are great for snacking or adding to salads, soups, or trail mixes.

Radish chips: Slice the radishes very thinly, about **1/16 inch (0.15 cm)** thick. Prepare and sprinkle them with some salt and paprika, and spread them in a single layer on the dehydrator trays. Dehydrate at **135°F (57°C)** for **5 to 7 hours**, or until crisp and dry. 1 pound (0.45 kg) of fresh radishes will yield about **2 oz (56 g)** of dried radish chips. They have a spicy and smoky flavor, a reddish color, and a crispy texture. They are delicious for munching on or serving with dips or cheese.

Radish tops and tails: The stem and root portion make a great addition to vegetable powder. Cut the stems and roots from the radishes and wash them well. Cut them into small pieces and spread them in a single layer on the dehydrator trays. Dehydrate at **125°F (52°C)** for **4 to 6 hours**, or until dry and hard. One pound (0.45 kg) of fresh radish tops and tails will yield about **1 ounce (28 g)** of dried radish tops and tails. They have a slightly bitter flavor, a brownish color, and a hard texture. They are good for grinding into a veggie powder for adding to soups, sauces, or smoothies.

Raspberries

How to choose

The best raspberries for dehydration are fresh, ripe, and firm. Avoid raspberries that are moldy, bruised, or overripe. You can also use frozen raspberries, but make sure to thaw them completely and drain the excess liquid before dehydrating. You can dehydrate any variety of raspberries, such as red, black, or golden. However, some varieties may have more seeds or less flavor than others.

How to prepare

Wash the raspberries gently under cold running water and pat them dry with a paper towel. Remove any stems, leaves, or damaged berries. Cut the raspberries in half or leave them whole, depending on your preference. Halving the raspberries will reduce the drying time and make them easier to eat, but whole raspberries will retain more shape and texture.

Optionally, you can pre-treat the raspberries with lemon juice, and honey to prevent browning and enhance the flavor. To do this, dip the raspberries in a solution of 1/4 cup of lemon juice and 2 cups of water, or drizzle them with honey.

Whole dried: You can dehydrate whole raspberries by placing them on the dehydrator trays with the opening facing down. Set the dehydrator to the lowest temperature setting, which is **95°F (35°C)** on most models, and dry for **24 hours or more**. You will get about **1/10 pound (45g)** of dried whole raspberries from 1 pound (454 g) of fresh raspberries. Whole dried raspberries have a dark red color and a wrinkled appearance. They have a sweet and tart flavor that is very concentrated and intense. They are delicious snacks on their own, or you can use them to make tea, smoothies, or baked goods.

Raspberry chips: These are thin and crisp pieces of raspberries that are dehydrated until they are crunchy. To make them, you need to cut fresh or frozen raspberries (thaw slightly) into halves or quarters, about **0.5 to 1 inch (1.27 to 2.54 cm)** in diameter. Place the raspberries on the dehydrator trays with some space between them. Spray them lightly with lemon juice to prevent browning and dry at **135°F (57°C)** for **10 to 12 hours**. You will get **1/4 pound (113 g)** of dried raspberry chips from 1 pound (454 g) of fresh raspberries1. Raspberry chips have a bright red color and a sweet and tart flavor. They are perfect for snacking, adding to cereal, or making trail mix.

Spinach

How to choose

- Spinach is available all year round, but the best time to buy it is in the spring and fall when it is in season and has the most flavor.

- Look for fresh spinach that has bright green leaves and crisp stems. Avoid spinach that has yellow, wilted, or slimy leaves, or brown spots[2].

- You can also use frozen spinach, which is already washed and chopped and can save you some time and effort. However, frozen spinach may have less flavor and texture than fresh spinach.

How to prepare

- If you are using fresh spinach, wash it well under running water to remove any dirt or grit. You can use a salad spinner or a kitchen towel to dry it off.

- Remove any damaged or wilted leaves and pick off any large stems. You can chop the spinach if you want, or leave it whole.

How to blanch

- Spinach does not need to be blanched or pre-cooked before dehydrating, as the heat will reduce the oxalic acid content, which can interfere with the absorption of nutrients.

- If you are using frozen spinach, thaw it completely and squeeze out the excess water. You can skip the washing and trimming steps.

Raw leaves: You can use Whole leaves, Cut them into thin strips, about **1/4 inch (0.6 cm)** wide, or chop them into small pieces, about **1/8 inch (0.3 cm)** wide. Wash and dry the spinach leaves and remove any large stems. Place them on the dehydrator trays in a thin layer, spreading them evenly. Dehydrate at **125°F (52°C)** for **3–6 hours** until the leaves are dry and brittle. You can expect to get about **1/2 cup (30 g)** of dried spinach from 1 pound (454 g) of fresh spinach. The dried spinach will have a slightly darker color and a more concentrated flavor. You can use it to make spinach flakes, add it to salads, sandwiches, dips, soups, stews, casseroles, or smoothies, or rehydrate it and use it as fresh spinach or omelets, or rehydrate it and use it as fresh spinach

Blanched leaves: Wash and dry the spinach leaves and remove any large stems. Blanch them in boiling water for 30 seconds, then plunge them into ice water to stop the cooking process. Drain and squeeze out the excess water. Place them on the dehydrator trays in a single layer, leaving some space for air circulation. Dehydrate at **125°F (52°C)** for **4–8 hours** until the leaves are dry and brittle. You can expect to get about **1/4 cup (15 g)** of dried spinach from 1 pound (454 g) of fresh spinach. The dried spinach will have a lighter color and a milder flavor. You can use it to make spinach powder, add it to soups, stews, casseroles, or smoothies, or rehydrate it and use it as fresh spinach

The difference between dehydrating blanched leaves and raw leaves is that blanching is a process of briefly immersing the leaves in boiling water before drying them. This helps to stop the enzyme activity that can cause undesirable changes in flavor, color, and texture during storage. Blanching also reduces the oxalic acid in greens, which can interfere with the absorption of some minerals. Raw leaves are dehydrated without any prior treatment, which may result in less stable and less nutritious dried products. However, some people prefer to dehydrate raw leaves because they believe that blanching destroys some of the vitamins and enzymes in the spinach.

Star fruit

How to choose

Look for star fruits that are firm, yellow, and have a slight green tinge on the edges. Avoid fruits that are brown, wrinkled, or have dark spots. Choose star fruits that are ripe or slightly underripe, as they will have more flavor and less moisture than overripe ones. Smell the star fruit and pick the ones that have a fragrant and fruity aroma.

How to prepare

Wash and scrub off any dirt from each star fruit. Cut the ends off each star fruit. Then, using a sharp knife or a mandolin, cut the bruised edges off each of the points along the length, if needed. Use the tip of a paring knife to remove all the seeds. Soak the star fruit slices in lemon water for about 10 minutes to prevent browning and add some manginess.

Star fruit chips: The texture of the chips is likely to be crispy and crunchy, while the flavor is sweet tart. Cut fruit into 1/4 or 1/8 inch. To prevent fruits from oxidizing, which causes them to turn brown, you can spray them directly with lemon juice using a spray bottle. Dehydrate at **125°F (52°C)** for **10 hours**. They are crunchy and sweet, with a yellow color and a star shape, a great idea for Christmas snacks. They can be eaten as a snack or added to granola, trail mix, or cereal. 1 pound of raw star fruit yields about **3 oz. (85 grams)** of dried chips.

Strawberries

How to choose

The best strawberries for dehydration are ripe, firm, and fresh. Avoid strawberries that are bruised, moldy, or overripe. You can use any variety of strawberries, but smaller ones will dry faster and retain more flavor. You can also use frozen strawberries, but make sure to thaw them completely and pat them dry before dehydrating.

How to prepare

To prepare strawberries for dehydration, you need to wash them, remove the stems and hulls, and slice them. You can slice them horizontally or vertically, depending on your preference. The thinner you slice them, the faster they will dry. Aim for slices that are about 1/4 inch thick. You can also sprinkle some honey or lemon juice on the slices to enhance their sweetness or tartness.

Strawberry chips: Cut fresh or frozen strawberries (thaw slightly) into equal-sized pieces, about **1/4 inch (0.64 cm)** thick. Place strawberries on mesh trays, leaving a little space between each slice. Put in a dehydrator and dry at **135 F (57 C)** for **8 to 10 hours**. You will get about **1/4 pound (113 g)** of dried strawberry chips from 1 pound (454 g) of fresh strawberries. Strawberry chips have a bright red color and a sweet and tangy flavor. They are great for snacking, adding to granola, or making trail mix.

Whole dried: These are whole strawberries that are dehydrated until they are shriveled and chewy. To make them, you need to wash and hull fresh or frozen strawberries (thawed) and pat them dry with a paper towel. You can leave them whole or cut them in half, depending on the size of the berries and your preference. Place the strawberries on the dehydrator trays with some space between them. Set the dehydrator to a low temperature, about **95 F (35 C)**. It will take about **24 hours** to fully dry the strawberries, but you should check them periodically and rotate the trays for even drying. Whole dried strawberries have a dark red color and a wrinkled appearance. They have a sweet and tart flavor that is very concentrated and intense. They are delicious snacks on their own, or you can use them to make tea, smoothies, or baked goods.

Sweet potatoes

How to choose

Choose sweet potatoes that are firm, smooth, and free of bruises or cracks. Avoid those that have sprouts, green spots, or signs of decay. Select sweet potatoes that are similar in size and shape, so they will dehydrate evenly. Wash and scrub the sweet potatoes well under running water to remove any dirt or residue.

How to prepare

Cut and soak the sweet potato slices. Fill a large bowl full of fresh, room-temperature water. Soak the sweet potato slices for one to two hours. The starch in the sweet potato will prevent moisture from escaping, but soaking will help remove some of the starch, leading to crispier sweet potato chips.

How to blanch

The most common way to pretreat vegetables is to blanch them for a few minutes, using either steam or boiling water. For sweet potatoes, you can steam-blanch them for 2-3 minutes, until nearly tender.

Another way to pretreat sweet potatoes is to bake them. Baking your sweet potatoes in the oven at 350ºF (177ºC) for about 20 minutes and then fully dehydrating them will yield a much better flavor and texture when they are rehydrated.

Sweet potato chips: These are thin slices of sweet potato that are about **1/16 inch (0.16 cm)** thick. Place the sweet potato rounds into a bowl, and drizzle with oil. Bake them in the oven at 350 º F (177 º C) for about 20 minutes, then dehydrate them at **145°F (63°C)** for **10 -12 hours** until they are dry and hard. From 1 pound (0.45 kg) of raw sweet potato, we can get about **4 ounces (113 grams)** of dried chips. They have a sweet and mild flavor, a bright orange color, and a crunchy texture. They can be eaten as a snack or added to salads, soups, or granola.

Sweet potato shreds: Shred the sweet potatoes using the large holes of a box grater. Blanch them in boiling water for 2-3 minutes, then dehydrate them at **125°F (52°C)** for **6-10 hours** until they are dry and fluffy. The dried shreds have a sweet and earthy flavor, a dark orange color, and a soft texture. They can be used to make pancakes, waffles, hash browns, fritters, or latkes by rehydrating them in hot water for 5 minutes.

Sweet potato cubes: Cut the sweet potatoes into cubes no larger than **1/2 inch (1.27 cm)**. Bake them in the oven at 350ºF (177ºC) for about 20 minutes, then dehydrate them at **125°F (52°C)** for **8-12 hours** until they are dry and hard. The dried cubes have a sweet and nutty flavor, a bright orange color, and a crunchy texture. They can be used to make soups, stews, curries, or casseroles by rehydrating them in boiling water for 10-15 minutes.

Swiss chard

How to choose

When selecting Swiss chard for dehydration, look for fresh, crisp, and undamaged leaves. Avoid wilted, yellowed, or bruised leaves. You can use any variety of Swiss chard, such as rainbow, red, or white. The color of the stems and veins will not affect the taste or nutrition of the dried product. You can also use homegrown or store-bought Swiss chard, as long as it is clean and organic.

How to prepare

Before dehydrating Swiss chard, you need to wash it thoroughly and remove any dirt or insects. You can also remove the stems and ribs if you prefer, or cut them into smaller pieces and dehydrate them separately.

How to blanch

Some people like to blanch the Swiss chard before dehydrating, as this can reduce the oxalate content and improve the color and texture of the dried leaves. To blanch Swiss chard, you need to boil it for about a minute and then plunge it into ice water. Drain and pat dry the leaves and stems before dehydrating.

Beet leaf chips or flakes: Cut the beet leaves into **2-inch (5 cm)** for chips and **1/4-inch (0.6 cm),** for flakes, discarding the stems. You can also remove the stems and use the whole leaves. Spread them on dehydrator trays in a single layer and dehydrate at **125°F (52°C)** for **4 to 6 hours** or until crisp. One pound (0.45 kg) of fresh beet leaves will yield about **2 ounces (57 g)** of dried chips. The chips will have a dark green color and a crunchy texture. They will retain some of the earthy and slightly bitter flavor of the fresh leaves. Beet leaf chips can be eaten as a snack or sprinkled on salads, soups, or casseroles for extra nutrition and crunch.

Beet leaf powder: Follow the same steps as for beet leaf chips, but blend the dried leaves in a blender or food processor until they form a fine powder. The powder will have a deep green color and a mild flavor. It can be used to add color and nutrients to smoothies, sauces, dips, breads, or pasta.

Tomatoes

How to choose

- Choose ripe, firm, and blemish-free tomatoes for dehydrating.
- You can use any variety of tomatoes, but plum tomatoes or cherry tomatoes are ideal because they have less water content and more flesh.
- Avoid overripe, soft, or bruised tomatoes, as they may spoil faster or produce uneven results.
- You can dehydrate any kind of tomatoes, but some types may work better than others. Some examples of good tomatoes for drying are Roma, paste, or plum tomatoes. You can also dehydrate cherry, grape, or heirloom tomatoes, but they may take longer and have more seeds and skin.

How to prepare:

Before you cut the tomatoes, you need to wash them and remove the stems. You can also peel the tomatoes if you prefer, as the skin can become tough and leathery when dried. To peel the tomatoes, you can dip them in boiling water for a few seconds, then plunge them in cold water and slip off the skins. You can remove some or all the seeds and gel from the inside of the tomatoes with a small spoon if you don't want them in your dried tomatoes.

Dehydrated tomato slices. Cut the tomatoes into thin slices about **1/4 inch (0.64 cm)** thick. Rinse them in cold water, then dry them with paper towels. Sprinkle them lightly with salt and any herbs or spices you like. Place them on a dehydrator tray in a single layer and dehydrate them at **135 °F (57 °C)** for **6-8 hours**, until they are dry and leathery. From 1 pound (0.45 kg) of raw tomatoes, you can get about **2 ounces (57 g)** of dehydrated slices. Dehydrated tomato slices have a deep red color and a chewy texture. They have a concentrated tomato flavor, which can vary depending on the seasonings you use. You can use them to make tomato powder, add them to soups, stews, casseroles, or salads, or rehydrate them in oil or water and use them as a topping or a side dish.

Dehydrated cherry tomatoes. Cut the cherry tomatoes in half. Rinse them in cold water, then dry them with paper towels. Sprinkle them lightly with salt and any herbs or spices you like. Place them on a dehydrator tray in a single layer, cut side up, and dehydrate at **135 °F (57 °C)** for 8-10 hours, until they are dry and shriveled. From **1 pound (0.45 kg)** of raw cherry tomatoes, you can get about **1.5 ounces (43 g)** of dehydrated cherry tomatoes. Dehydrated cherry tomatoes are crunchy but they stay pleasantly chewy with a sweet flavor. You can use them to make tomato powder, add them to pasta, pizza, omelets, or cheese boards, or rehydrate them in oil or water and use them as a topping or a side dish.

Turnips

How to choose

Choose fresh, firm, and ripe turnips that are free of bruises, cracks, or soft spots. You can use any variety of turnips, but smaller ones tend to have a sweeter and milder flavor than larger ones.

How to prepare

Wash the turnips well under running water and peel them. You can also scrub them with a vegetable brush to remove any dirt or debris. Even if you are going to peel the turnips, it is worth washing them first to avoid spreading any dirt on the peeler or the flesh.

How to blanch

Blanch the turnip slices for 3 minutes in boiling water or steam. This will help preserve the color, flavor, and nutrients of the turnips, as well as prevent them from browning or spoiling. To blanch in water, drop the slices into a pot of boiling water and start timing once the water returns to a boil. To blanch in steam, place the slices in a steamer basket over a pot of boiling water, cover, and start timing once the steam is full. After 3 minutes, drain the turnip slices and cool them quickly in cold water or ice water. This will stop the cooking process and prevent them from becoming mushy.

Turnip chips: Cut the turnips into thin slices, about **1/8 inch (3.2 mm)** thick. Arrange the turnip slices on the dehydrator trays in a single layer, leaving some space between them. Season the turnip slices with salt, pepper, or any other seasoning of your choice. Dry for one hour at **150°F (65°C)**. Reduce the heat to **135°F (57°C)** and dry the turnip slices for about 4 hours, or until they are crisp and brittle. You can get about 1/4 pound (113 g) of turnip chips from **1 pound (454 g)** of raw turnips. Turnip chips have a light yellow color and a crunchy texture. They have a mild and slightly sweet flavor, similar to potato chips. You can eat turnip chips as a snack, or use them as a garnish for soups and salads.

Turnip powder: Cut the turnips into small pieces, about **1/4 inch (6.4 mm)** in size. Arrange the turnip pieces on the dehydrator trays in a single layer, leaving some space between them. Set the dehydrator to **145°F (63°C)** and dry the turnip pieces for about 6 hours, or until they are hard and dry. You can get about **1/8 pound (57 g)** of turnip powder from 1 pound (454 g) of raw turnips. Turnip powder has a white color and a fine texture. It has a mild and slightly bitter flavor, similar to fresh turnips. You can use turnip powder to thicken soups and sauces or to add flavor and nutrition to smoothies and baked goods.

Turnip jerky: Cut the turnips into thin strips, about **1/4 inch (6.4 mm)** thick and **2 inch (5.1 cm)** long. Marinate the turnip strips in a mixture of soy sauce, honey, garlic, ginger, and any other spices of your choice for at least 2 hours in the refrigerator. Drain the turnip strips and arrange them on the dehydrator trays in a single layer, leaving some space between them. Set the dehydrator to **160°F (71°C)** and dry the turnip strips for about 6-8 hours, or until they are chewy and leathery. You can get about 1/4 pound (113 g) of turnip jerky from **1 pound (454 g)** of raw turnips. Turnip jerky has a dark brown color and a chewy texture. It has a savory and slightly sweet flavor, similar to meat jerky. You can eat turnip jerky as a snack, or use it as a protein source in salads and sandwiches.

Watermelon

How to choose

Choose a watermelon that has a uniform and symmetrical shape without dents, cracks, or damage. Irregularities may indicate improper watering or pollination of the watermelon. Lift the watermelon and feel its weight. It should be heavy for its size, which means it is full of water and juicy. Turn the watermelon over and look at the spot where it lay on the ground. This spot should be creamy yellow or orange, which indicates that the watermelon ripened on the vine. If the spot is white or light yellow, the watermelon may be underripe and not sweet. Tap on the watermelon and listen to the sound it makes. If the sound is dull and resonant, the watermelon has more water and is riper. If the sound is high and dense, it may mean that the rind of the watermelon is too thick, and the watermelon is not fully ripe.

How to prepare

Before cutting the watermelon, wash it well and dry it. This will help avoid contaminating the flesh with bacteria from the surface of the watermelon. Cut the watermelon in half and then into quarters. Carefully cut out the flesh from the rind with a sharp knife. If the watermelon has large black seeds, remove them from the flesh. White seeds can be left, but they will not affect the taste.

Watermelon chips: These are thin and crispy watermelon pieces with a sweet and refreshing taste. They are perfect for a snack or a dessert. To make: Slice the watermelon into thin slices, about **1/8 inch** thick. Dry the watermelon at **135°F (57°C)** for **8-12 hours**, turning the slices every 2 hours. Watermelon chips are ready when it becomes crunchy and easy to break. Light pink color and fragrant smell. You will get about **0.1 pounds (45 g)** of watermelon chips from 1 pound of fresh watermelon.

Watermelon candy. These are soft and chewy pieces of watermelon that have an intense and sweet taste. They are similar to jelly or marmalade, but without adding sugar or gelatin. To make: Cut the watermelon into cubes, about **1/2 inch by 1/2 inch**. Dry the watermelon at **135°F (57°C)** for **12-16 hours**, turning the cubes every 4 hours. Watermelon candy is ready when it becomes soft and chewy, but not sticky. It will have a dark pink color and a sweet smell. You will get about **0.2 pounds (90 g)** of watermelon candy from 1 pound of fresh watermelon.

Zucchini

How to choose

Select fresh zucchini that are firm, smooth, and have a vibrant green color. They should be free of blemishes and not too large, as oversized zucchini can be watery and have large seeds. Smaller, younger zucchini tend to have better flavor and texture for dehydration. Avoid zucchini that are soft, wrinkled, or have discolored spots, as these are signs of age and may not dehydrate well.

How to prepare

Wash the zucchini thoroughly under cold water to remove any dirt or debris. Trim off the ends and slice the zucchini into uniform rounds or strips. A mandolin slicer can help achieve consistent thickness.

How to blanch

Blanching zucchini before dehydrating can help to preserve their color and texture. Bring a large pot of water to a rolling boil. Add the zucchini slices and blanch for 1 to 2 minutes. Immediately transfer the blanched zucchini to a bowl of ice water to stop the cooking process and maintain its bright green color. Drain the zucchini well and pat them dry with a clean kitchen towel or paper towel to remove excess moisture.

Zucchini chips: Prepare and cut the zucchini into **1/8 inch (0.3 cm)** rounds using a knife or a mandolin. Arrange the zucchini slices on the dehydrator trays in a single layer, leaving some space between them. Dehydrate at around **140°F (60°C)**. It typically takes between **4 and 6 hours**, depending on the moisture content of the zucchini and the humidity of your environment. They should be crisp and brittle, not soft or chewy. If they are not done, continue drying until they are. 1 pound (0.45 kg) of fresh zucchini will yield about **1.5 ounces (42 g)** of zucchini chips.

Zucchini noodles: These are long strands of zucchini that resemble pasta noodles. They are also known as zoodles or zucchini spaghetti. Cut the zucchini and peel them if you prefer. Peeling is optional, but it will make the noodles more uniform and texture. Use a spiralizer, a julienne peeler, or a vegetable peeler to create thin and long zucchini noodles. You can also use a knife to cut the zucchini into thin strips, but this will take more time and effort. Spread the zucchini noodles on the dehydrator trays in a single layer, separating them as much as possible. Dehydrate at around **135°F (57°C)** and start the dehydrating process. It usually takes about 6 to 8 hours, depending on the thickness of the noodles and the humidity of your environment. They should be pliable and dry, not moist or brittle. If they are not done, continue drying until they are. 1 pound (0.45 kg) of fresh zucchini will yield about **2 ounces (56 g)** of zucchini noodles. Zucchini noodles are soft and tender when rehydrated, and they have a mild and slightly sweet flavor. They can be used as a substitute for pasta in various dishes, such as salads, soups, casseroles, stir-fries, and more.

Zucchini cubes: Cut the zucchini into **1/2 inch (1.3 cm)** cubes using a knife or a food chopper. Prepare and spread the zucchini cubes on the dehydrator trays in a single layer, leaving some space between them. Dehydrate at around **125°F (52°C)**. It usually takes about **8 to 10 hours**, depending on the moisture content of the zucchini and the humidity of your environment. They should be hard and dry and can be slightly chewy but not soft or moist. 1 pound (0.45 kg) of fresh zucchini will yield about **2 ounces (56 g)** of zucchini cubes.

Zucchini cubes are firm and chewy when dried, and they have a mild and slightly earthy flavor. They can be rehydrated by soaking them in water or broth for about 15 minutes, or by adding them directly to soups, stews, or other dishes that have enough liquid. They can also be eaten as a snack or added to salads for a crunchy texture.

Meat, Fish, and Seafood

Fish

Dehydrating fish is a great way to preserve it and enjoy it later. Dehydrated fish can be used in soups, stews, salads, or snacks. It can also add a rich flavor and texture to your dishes. In this article, we will show you how to choose and prepare fish for dehydration.

How to choose

The best fish for dehydration are lean, firm, and fresh. Lean fish have less fat and moisture, which makes them easier to dry and store. Firm fish have a dense and meaty texture, which holds up well during the dehydration process. Fresh fish have a mild and pleasant flavor, which is enhanced by the seasoning and drying.

Some examples of lean and firm fish are cod, haddock, halibut, pollack, bass, sole, trout, and tuna. Lean fish are easier to dry and store because they have less fat and moisture. Fat fish can still be dehydrated, but they may take longer to dry and have a shorter shelf life. Salmon is a popular choice for dehydration because it has a firm texture and a rich flavor. You can use any type of fish that you like, if it is fresh and properly prepared. Check the storage conditions in the 'Storage' section.

How to prepare

Before dehydrating fish, you need to prepare it by cutting, seasoning, and curing it. Here are the steps to follow:

- Begin by cleaning the perch thoroughly. Remove the fins, gills, and any sharp protruding parts to avoid injuring yourself during the process. Rinse the fish under cold water to remove any dirt or debris.
- After cleaning, pat the fish dry with paper towels. This step is crucial as excess moisture can hinder the dehydration process. Ensure both the fish and your workspace are dry.
- Cut the fish into thin slices. You can cut the fish along or across the grain, depending on your preference. The thinner the slices, the faster they will dry.

- Cure the fish by soaking it in a brine solution for a few hours or overnight. Brining helps to draw out the moisture and prevent bacterial growth. A basic brine solution consists of water, salt, and sugar, but you can also add other ingredients such as vinegar, lemon juice, or wine. The ratio of water to salt and sugar is usually 4 cups of water to 1/4 cup of salt and 1/4 cup of sugar. You can adjust the amount of salt and sugar according to your taste and the type of fish you are using.
- Rinse the fish and pat it dry with paper towels.
- You can also blot off any excess seasoning or marinade if you wish.
- Be careful not to over-season the fish, as the flavor will intensify during the drying process.

Fish Strips: These are thin and crispy strips of fish that are great for snacking or adding to salads. To make them, you need to slice the fish into **1/4 inch (6 mm)** strips and marinate them in your choice of seasonings for up to 12 hours in the refrigerator. Pat the fish strips dry, and place them in a single layer on dehydrator trays. Set the food dehydrator to **145°F (63°C)** and dry the fish for **10 to 12 hours**, or until they are firm, dry, and pliable. If they still feel moist, continue drying until they are crisp. One pound (454 g) of fresh fish will yield about **4 ounces (113 g)** of fish strips. To check for doneness, break a strip in half and look for any signs of moisture. If the strip is still soft, it needs more drying time. Fish strips have a savory and salty taste and a golden color. They are crunchy and chewy and can be stored in an airtight container for up to 3 months.

Fish Jerky: This is a thick and chewy snack that is made by seasoning and dehydrating fish fillets. To make it, you need to cut the fish into **1/2 inch (1.3 cm)** thick slices and marinate them in your choice of seasonings for up to 24 hours in the refrigerator. Pat the fish slices dry, and place them in a single layer on dehydrator trays. Set the dehydrator to **160°F (71°C)** and dry the fish for **12 to 16 hours**, or until they are dry and leathery. They should still be a bit pliable, but not moist or sticky. One pound (454 g) of fresh fish will yield about **6 ounces (170 g)** of fish jerky. To check for doneness, bend a slice and look for any signs of moisture. If the slice breaks easily, it is over-dried. If the slice is still moist, it needs more drying time. It is thick and chewy and can be stored in an airtight container for up to 6 months.

Fish Flakes: This is a light and flaky snack that is made by dehydrating fish fillets and breaking them into small pieces. To make it, you need to cook the fish in water or broth until it flakes easily with a fork. Drain the fish and flake it with a fork or a food processor. You can also add some seasonings, such as salt, pepper, garlic, or herbs, to enhance the flavor. Spread the flaked fish on dehydrator trays and dehydrate at **135°F (57°C)** for **6 to 8 hours**, or until the fish is dry and crumbly. One pound (454 g) of fresh fish will yield about **2 cups (100 g)** of fish flakes. To check for doneness, crumble a piece of fish and look for any signs of moisture. If the piece is still moist, it needs more drying time. Fish flakes have a mild and delicate taste. They are light and flaky and can be stored in an airtight container for up to 6 months. You can use fish flakes to make fish cakes, fish pies, fish salads, or fish soups.

Meat

How to choose and prepare

Choose fresh, high-quality meat that has been properly handled and stored. Avoid meat that has been frozen and thawed multiple times, as this can affect its texture and flavor.

The best meat for dehydration is lean and low in fat, such as beef, chicken, turkey, and ham. Choose tender cuts of meat, as they will be less chewy or tough after dehydrating. Some good choices for beef are top round, bottom round, sirloin, or flank steak. Trim off any visible fat before dehydrating.

Fatty meats can go rancid quickly and affect the taste and quality of the dehydrated product. Anticipating your question, yes, you can dehydrate pork or duck, as long as you follow the proper food safety guidelines. Pork and duck are both high in fat, which can make them prone to spoilage and rancidity. You should trim off any excess fat before dehydrating, and rinse the meat with hot water to remove any oil and blot off any oil during the process. Some of the cuts of pork and duck that are suitable for dehydration are pork loin, pork belly, and duck breast: Pork loin is a lean and tender cut of pork that can be dehydrated into jerky, strips, cubes, flakes, or crumbles.

Cook the meat before or after dehydrating, to ensure that it reaches a safe internal temperature of 160°F (71°C) for beef and 165°F (74°C) for poultry. You can either boil the meat in the marinade or bake it in the oven before dehydrating, or heat it in the oven for 10 minutes at 275°F (135°C) after dehydrating.

Food Safety Recommendations for working with raw meat

If you want to make homemade jerky, you should follow the advice, which is based on scientific research. They recommend that you always use safe practices when handling and preparing meat products, such as:

- Washing your hands with soap and water for at least 20 seconds before and after touching any raw meat or poultry.
- Using clean and sanitized cutting boards, knives, and other utensils to prevent cross-contamination.
- To avoid accidents, use a sharp knife instead of a dull one. Fat can make your knife lose its edge fast, so have a knife sharpener handy to keep it in good shape. A sharp knife will cut smoothly and not slide off, which could hurt you.
- Throw away the marinade when you are done. Do not use it again.
- Storing meat and poultry in the coldest part of the refrigerator and using or freezing them within the recommended time frame: 2 days for ground beef and poultry, and 3 to 5 days for whole cuts of red meat.
- Thawing frozen meat in the refrigerator, not at room temperature, to prevent the growth of harmful bacteria.

- Marinating meat in the refrigerator, not on the counter, and discarding any leftover marinade. Marinades help to make the jerky more tender and flavorful, but they can also contain harmful bacteria if not handled properly.

- For easier cutting, use slightly frozen meat, either before it has fully defrosted or put it back in the freezer for 1–2 hours to harden a bit. This will help keep the piece of meat steady for more even and safe cutting (the meat won't be sliding around as much).

- When cutting your pieces, cut with the grain for a chewier jerky (harder to bite, often longer pieces). Cut across the grain for a more tender jerky (easier to chew).

- Cooking meat to a safe internal temperature before dehydrating it: 160°F (71°C) for beef, pork, lamb, and veal, and 165°F (74°C) for chicken and turkey. You can check the temperature with a food thermometer inserted into the thickest part of the meat.

- Drying meat in a food dehydrator that can reach and maintain a temperature of at least 130°F (54°C) to 145°F (62°C) throughout the drying process. This ensures that the jerky is dried enough to prevent spoilage and kill any remaining bacteria.

- If you want to dehydrate different types of meat such as chicken and beef at the same time, you should use separate trays and check them periodically for doneness. Chicken may take longer to dry than beef, depending on the thickness and seasoning of the slices.

- You should also blot off any excess oil or fat with paper towels once or twice while drying, as this can prevent spoilage and improve the texture of the dehydrated meat.

Let's consider a few ideas that focus on classic types of dehydrated meat such as jerky, strips, flakes, cubes, and crumbles. You can use any meat for each recipe and make your own experiments.

Meat jerky: This is a popular snack made from thin slices of lean meat that are marinated and dried until chewy. You can use beef, turkey, venison, or any other game meat for this. Cut the meat into **1/4 inch (0.6 cm)** thick slices across the grain and marinate with your choice of seasonings for 2 to 4 hours. Some common ingredients for the marinade are soy sauce, Worcestershire sauce, salt, pepper, garlic, onion, brown sugar, and liquid smoke. Dehydrate the meat at **145°F (63°C)** for **4 to 6 hours**, flipping halfway through. Blot off any fat with paper towels once or twice while drying. You will get about **1/4 pound (113 g)** of dried product from 1 pound (454 g) of raw meat. The jerky will have a dark brown color, a chewy texture, and a savory flavor. You can eat it as a snack or add it to soups and stews.

Meat strips: This is like jerky, but the meat is cut into thicker and longer strips that are more tender and moister. You can use beef, pork, chicken, or any other meat for this. Cut the meat into **1/2 inch (1.3 cm)** thick slices along the grain and season with salt, pepper, and any other spices you like. You can also use a dry rub or a wet marinade for more flavor. Dehydrate the meat at **140°F (60°C)** for **6 to 8 hours**, flipping halfway through. You will get about **1/3 pound (151 g)** of dried product from 1 pound (454 g) of raw meat. The meat strips will have a light golden color, a tender texture, and a mild flavor. You can eat them as a snack or rehydrate them with water or broth and use them in salads, sandwiches, and casseroles.

Meat flakes: This is a way to dehydrate cooked meat that has been shredded or chopped into small pieces. You can use beef, chicken, turkey, ham, or any other meat for this. Cook the meat until tender and then shred or chop it into **1/4 inch (0.6 cm)** pieces. Season with salt, pepper, and any other herbs or spices you like. You can also add some broth or sauce to moisten the meat. Dehydrate the meat at **145°F (63°C)** for **4 to 6 hours**, stirring occasionally. You will get about **1/2 pound (227 g)** of dried product from 1 pound (454 g) of raw meat. The meat flakes will have a pinkish-red color, a crumbly texture, and a salty flavor. You can use them in soups, stews, omelets, and pasta dishes.

Meat cubes: This is a way to dehydrate cooked meat that has been cut into small cubes. You can use beef, chicken, pork, or any other meat for this. Cook the meat until done and then cut it into 1/2 inch (1.3 cm) cubes. Season with salt, pepper, and any other spices you like. You can also add some broth or sauce to coat the meat. Dehydrate the meat at **140°F (60°C)** for **6 to 8 hours**, stirring occasionally. You will get about **1/3 pound (151 g)** of dried product from 1 pound (454 g) of raw meat. The meat cubes will have a light golden color, a crunchy texture, and a mild flavor. You can eat them as a snack or rehydrate them with water or broth and use them in salads, sandwiches, and casseroles.

Meat crumbles: This is a way to dehydrate ground meat that has been cooked and drained. You can use beef, turkey, pork, or any other meat for this. Cook the meat in a skillet over medium-high heat until browned and cooked through. Drain the fat and season with salt, pepper, and any other spices you like. You can also add some broth or sauce to flavor the meat. Dehydrate the meat at **145°F (63°C)** for **4 to 6 hours**, breaking up any clumps with a fork. You will get about **1/4 pound (113 g)** of dried product from 1 pound (454 g) of raw meat. The meat crumbles will have a dark brown color, a granular texture, and a savory flavor. You can use them in tacos, burritos, chili, and pizza.

20 Best Marinades for Dehydrating Meat

Teriyaki marinade: Combine 1/4 cup of soy sauce, 2 tablespoons of brown sugar, 2 tablespoons of honey, 1 tablespoon of grated ginger, 2 cloves of minced garlic, and 1 teaspoon of sesame oil in a bowl. This marinade is great for beef, chicken, or turkey jerky.

BBQ marinade: Combine 1/4 cup of ketchup, 2 tablespoons of brown sugar, 2 tablespoons of apple cider vinegar, 1 tablespoon of Worcestershire sauce, 1 teaspoon of mustard, 1/2 teaspoon of garlic powder, 1/2 teaspoon of onion powder, and 1/4 teaspoon of smoked paprika in a bowl. This marinade is perfect for beef, pork, or chicken strips.

Spicy marinade: Combine 1/4 cup of soy sauce, 2 tablespoons of hot sauce, 2 tablespoons of honey, 2 tablespoons of lime juice, 1 teaspoon of cumin, 1 teaspoon of chili powder, and 1/4 teaspoon of garlic powder in a bowl. This marinade is ideal for beef, chicken, or turkey jerky.

Lemon pepper marinade: Combine 1/4 cup of lemon juice, 2 tablespoons of soy sauce, 2 tablespoons of olive oil, 1 tablespoon of honey, 2 teaspoons of black pepper, and 1/4 teaspoon of garlic powder in a bowl. This marinade is suitable for beef, chicken, or turkey strips.

Honey garlic marinade: Combine 1/4 cup of honey, 2 tablespoons of soy sauce, 2 tablespoons of apple cider vinegar, 2 cloves of minced garlic, and 1/4 teaspoon of black pepper in a bowl. This marinade is delicious for beef, chicken, or pork jerky.

Smoky maple marinade: Combine 1/4 cup of maple syrup, 2 tablespoons of soy sauce, 2 tablespoons of liquid smoke, 1 tablespoon of apple cider vinegar, 1/2 teaspoon of garlic powder, and 1/4 teaspoon of black pepper in a bowl. This marinade is amazing for beef, pork, or turkey jerky.

Asian marinade: Combine 1/4 cup of soy sauce, 2 tablespoons of rice vinegar, 2 tablespoons of hoisin sauce, 1 tablespoon of sesame oil, 1 tablespoon of brown sugar, 1 tablespoon of grated ginger, 2 cloves of minced garlic, and 1/4 teaspoon of red pepper flakes in a bowl. This marinade is wonderful for beef, chicken, or pork jerky.

Italian marinade: Combine 1/4 cup of olive oil, 2 tablespoons of balsamic vinegar, 2 tablespoons of lemon juice, 2 teaspoons of dried oregano, 2 teaspoons of dried basil, 1 teaspoon of salt, 1/2 teaspoon of black pepper, and 2 cloves of minced garlic in a bowl. This marinade is excellent for beef, chicken, or turkey strips.

Moroccan marinade: Combine 1/4 cup of olive oil, 2 tablespoons of lemon juice, 2 tablespoons of honey, 2 teaspoons of cumin, 2 teaspoons of paprika, 1 teaspoon of salt, 1/2 teaspoon of cinnamon, 1/4 teaspoon of cayenne pepper, and 2 cloves of minced garlic in a bowl. This marinade is exotic for beef, chicken, or turkey cubes.

Greek marinade: Combine 1/4 cup of plain yogurt, 2 tablespoons of olive oil, 2 tablespoons of lemon juice, 2 teaspoons of dried oregano, 1 teaspoon of salt, 1/2 teaspoon of black pepper, and 2 cloves of minced garlic in a bowl. This marinade is refreshing for beef, chicken, or turkey cubes.

Mexican marinade: Combine 1/4 cup of lime juice, 2 tablespoons of vegetable oil, 2 tablespoons of chopped cilantro, 2 teaspoons of chili powder, 1 teaspoon of cumin, 1 teaspoon of salt, 1/2 teaspoon of oregano, and 1/4 teaspoon of garlic powder in a bowl. This marinade is zesty for beef, chicken, or turkey strips.

Indian marinade: Combine 1/4 cup of plain yogurt, 2 tablespoons of vegetable oil, 2 tablespoons of lemon juice, 2 teaspoons of Garam masala, 2 teaspoons of turmeric, 1 teaspoon of salt, 1/2 teaspoon of cumin, 1/4 teaspoon of ginger, and 1/4 teaspoon of garlic powder in a bowl. This marinade is spicy for beef, chicken, or turkey cubes.

Cajun marinade: Combine 1/4 cup of vegetable oil, 2 tablespoons of apple cider vinegar, 2 tablespoons of Worcestershire sauce, 2 teaspoons of paprika, 2 teaspoons of garlic powder, 1 teaspoon of salt, 1 teaspoon of onion powder, 1/2 teaspoon of black pepper, 1/2 teaspoon of thyme, 1/4 teaspoon of cayenne pepper, and 1/4 teaspoon of oregano in a bowl. This marinade is fiery for beef, chicken, or pork strips.

Hawaiian marinade: Combine 1/4 cup of pineapple juice, 2 tablespoons of soy sauce, 2 tablespoons of brown sugar, 1 tablespoon of ketchup, 1 tablespoon of rice vinegar, 1 teaspoon of liquid smoke, and 1/4 teaspoon of ginger in a bowl. This marinade is tropical for beef, chicken, or pork jerky.

Rosemary garlic marinade: Combine 1/4 cup of olive oil, 2 tablespoons of red wine vinegar, 2 tablespoons of chopped rosemary, 2 cloves of minced garlic, 1 teaspoon of salt, and 1/2 teaspoon of black pepper in a bowl. This marinade is aromatic for beef, chicken, or turkey strips.

Bourbon marinade: Combine 1/4 cup of bourbon, 2 tablespoons of soy sauce, 2 tablespoons of brown sugar, 1 tablespoon of Worcestershire sauce, 1 tablespoon of Dijon mustard, 1/4 teaspoon of garlic powder, and 1/4 teaspoon of black pepper in a bowl. This marinade is boozy for beef, pork, or chicken jerky.

Thai marinade: Combine 1/4 cup of coconut milk, 2 tablespoons of fish sauce, 2 tablespoons of lime juice, 2 tablespoons of brown sugar, 1 tablespoon of soy sauce, 1 tablespoon of chopped cilantro, 1 teaspoon of curry powder, and 1/4 teaspoon of red pepper flakes in a bowl. This marinade is tangy for beef, chicken, or pork jerky.

Ranch marinade: Combine 1/4 cup of buttermilk, 2 tablespoons of mayonnaise, 2 tablespoons of sour cream, 2 teaspoons of dried parsley, 1 teaspoon of dried dill, 1 teaspoon of garlic powder, 1 teaspoon of onion powder, 1/2 teaspoon of salt, and 1/4 teaspoon of black pepper in a bowl. This marinade is creamy for beef, chicken, or turkey strips.

Jamaican marinade: Combine 1/4 cup of vegetable oil, 2 tablespoons of lime juice, 2 tablespoons of soy sauce, 2 teaspoons of brown sugar, 2 teaspoons of allspice, 1 teaspoon of thyme, 1/2 teaspoon of salt, 1/4 teaspoon of nutmeg, 1/4 teaspoon of cinnamon, and 1/4 teaspoon of cayenne pepper in a bowl. This marinade is flavorful for beef, chicken, or pork cubes.

Balsamic marinade: Combine 1/4 cup of balsamic vinegar, 2 tablespoons of olive oil, 2 tablespoons of honey, 1 tablespoon of soy sauce, 1 teaspoon of dried rosemary, 1/2 teaspoon of salt, and 1/4 teaspoon of black pepper in a bowl. This marinade is sweet for beef, chicken, or turkey jerky.

Wild Game Food Safety

There are some special considerations for making jerky from wild game, such as venison, elk, or moose. According to the USDA, wild game meat may contain parasites or bacteria that can cause foodborne illness, so it is important to handle and cook it properly. Some of the tips for making safe and tasty wild game jerky are:

Freeze the meat for at least 30 days at 0°F (-18°C) before dehydrating, to kill any parasites that may be present.

Defrost safety:

- There are a few defrosting methods that are safe for making jerky. Put them in the fridge to defrost. Make sure to put them in a bowl, tub, plate, or cooking sheet with rims, etc. to catch any liquid during the defrosting process. For whole parts of the animal that are 2–3 pounds each, this will probably take 2–3 days to fully defrost. Remember: raw wild game should go on the lowest shelf possible in your fridge!

- Put them under cool, running water. Water should be about 70 F, which feels pretty cold with your bare hands. Do not put them under hot, running water. For large parts of the animal, this can take a long time and use a lot of water.

- The other defrosting methods (microwaving etc.) are not suggested for this, as jerky will not be cooked and eaten right away after defrosting.

- Trim off any fat, gristle, or connective tissue from the meat, as they can spoil faster and affect the flavor and texture of the jerky.

- Cook the meat before or after dehydrating, to ensure that it reaches a safe internal temperature register of 165°F (74°C) when using a calibrated food thermometer.

- You can either boil the meat in the marinade or bake it in the oven before dehydrating, or heat it in the oven for 10 minutes at 275°F (135°C) after dehydrating.

Seafood & Shellfish

Dehydrated shellfish can be used as a snack, a seasoning, or an ingredient for soups, stews, salads, and other dishes. The following steps and tips are general guidelines for dehydrating different types of seafood. You can adjust them according to your preference and the availability of the seafood. You can use any lean shellfish, such as oysters, shrimp, lobster, clam, crab, and scallops, squid, mussels, octopus, and caviar. You can also experiment with different seasonings, marinades, and drying methods to create your unique flavors and textures:

How to choose

Choosing fresh and high-quality shellfish is important for dehydration, as it affects the flavor, texture, and shelf life of the final product. Here are some tips on how to choose shellfish for dehydration:

- Give the shellfish a sniff. It should have a nice, clean ocean smell. The briny smell of saltwater is good, but avoid anything that smells sour or overly fishy.

- Look at the color and appearance of the shellfish. It should be bright, shiny, and moist. Avoid any shellfish that looks dull, dry, or slimy.

- Check the shells of the shellfish. They should be tightly closed or closed when tapped. Avoid any shellfish that have cracked, broken, or open shells.

- Ask the fishmonger or seller about the source and freshness of the shellfish. Choose shellfish that are caught or harvested from clean and sustainable waters. Prefer shellfish that are caught or harvested on the same day or the day before. Avoid any shellfish that are more than two days old.

How to blanch

Some shellfish, such as shrimp, lobster, and crab, have to be blanched before dehydration. This is because they are high in protein and fat, which can make them prone to rancidity and spoilage. Blanching helps to remove some of the fat and prevent oxidation.

Other shellfish, such as oysters, mussels, and clams, do not need to be blanched before dehydration, but you still can blanch them if you wish. This is because they are low in fat and have a high moisture content, which makes them dry faster and more evenly. However, they must be shelled and washed before dehydration.

To blanch shellfish, bring a large pot of water to a boil and add some salt and vinegar. The salt helps to season the shellfish and the vinegar helps to prevent discoloration. Then, add the shellfish and boil for a few minutes, depending on the size and type of the shellfish. You can use a timer or a thermometer to check the doneness of the shellfish. The shellfish should be cooked but not overcooked. Then, drain the shellfish and plunge them into ice water to stop the cooking process. Drain again and pat dry with paper towels. Then, you can proceed to dehydrate the shellfish according to your preferred method.

Here are some ideas of recipes for shellfish such as oysters, shrimp, lobster, clam, crab, scallops, squid, mussel, octopus, and caviar:

Shellfish jerky: Shellfish jerky is a type of dehydrated seafood that has a tough texture and a sweet and savory flavor. It can be eaten as a snack or chopped and added to salads and sandwiches. To make shellfish jerky, you need to cut the shellfish into **1/4 inch (6 mm)** thick slices or strips. You can use shrimp, lobster, crab, or any other lean shellfish. Marinate them in a mixture of soy sauce, brown sugar, garlic, ginger, and pepper for up to 12 hours in the refrigerator. Rinse and place them on a dehydrator tray in a single layer. Dry at **145°F (63°C)** for **12 hours**, or until dry and leathery. You can get about **4 ounces (113 grams)** of shellfish jerky from 1 pound (454 grams) of fresh shellfish.

Shellfish powder: Shellfish powder is a type of dehydrated seafood that has a smooth texture and a mild and nutty flavor. It can be used as a seasoning for soups, sauces, dips, and dressings. To make shellfish powder, you need to grind the shellfish in a food processor or blender until they form a paste. You can use shrimp, lobster, crab, or any other lean shellfish. Spread the paste thinly and evenly on a parchment paper-lined dehydrator tray. Dry at **125°F (52°C)** for **10 hours**, or until brittle. Break the dried paste into pieces and grind them again in a blender or spice grinder until they form a fine powder. You can get about **2 ounces (57 grams)** of shellfish powder from 1 pound (454 grams) of fresh shellfish.

Shellfish chips: Shellfish chips are a type of dehydrated seafood that has a crunchy texture and a salty and briny flavor. They can be eaten as a snack or served with dips and salsa. To make shellfish chips, you need to cut the shellfish into thin slices, about **1/8 inch (3 mm)** thick. You can use shrimp, lobster, crab, scallops, or any other lean shellfish. Sprinkle some salt and pepper on both sides of the slices. Place them on a dehydrator tray in a single layer. Dry at **135°F (57°C)** for **8 hours**, or until crisp. You can get about **5 ounces (142 grams)** of shellfish chips from 1 pound (454 grams) of fresh shellfish.

Shellfish flakes: Shellfish flakes are a type of dehydrated seafood that has a flaky texture and a mild and sweet flavor. They can be used as a topping for salads, pasta, pizza, and baked dishes. To make shellfish flakes, you need to cut the shellfish into small pieces, about **1/4 inch (6 mm)** in size. You can use shrimp, lobster, crab, clam, mussels, or any other lean shellfish. Place them on a dehydrator tray in a single layer. Dry at **140°F (60°C)** for **10 hours**, or until dry and flaky. You can get about **4 ounces (113 grams)** of shellfish flakes from 1 pound (454 grams) of fresh shellfish.

Bread

How to choose

Choosing the right bread for dehydration depends on your preference and the purpose of the dehydrated bread. Here are some general tips to help you select the best bread. The best bread for dehydration varies depending on what you want to use the dehydrated bread for and what kind of taste and texture you like. However, some general tips to keep in mind are: First, stale or refrigerated bread is better than fresh bread, because it dries faster and does not clump together. Second, non-oily breads, such as sourdough, rye, or homemade bread, are better than oily breads, such as brioche or croissants, because they do not go rancid quickly and they dry well. Third, whole-grain or enriched breads are better than breads with added sugars because they provide more fiber and nutrients, as well as iron, folate, and B vitamins. Fourth, you can use any bread you like to make different kinds of dehydrated bread products, such as breadcrumbs, croutons, stuffing mix, cake, or bread pudding, and you can season them with your favorite herbs, spices, oil, cheese, or other ingredients before dehydrating them.

How to choose and prepare

Refrigerate the bread you want to dehydrate overnight or use stale bread. This will help the bread dry faster and prevent clumping. Decide whether you want to make breadcrumbs or bread cubes. Breadcrumbs are good for baking or coating, while bread cubes are good for croutons or stuffing. To make breadcrumbs, pulse the bread in a food processor or blender. To make bread cubes, slice the bread into slices or cubes. Spread the breadcrumbs or cubes on dehydrator trays. You can use parchment paper, fruit leather sheets, or lipped trays to prevent the bread from falling through the gaps. You can use frozen bread for dehydration, as long as you thaw it first. Frozen bread can be reheated in the oven at 350°F (175°C) for 10–15 minutes until it is soft and crispy. Then, you can slice or cube the bread and dehydrate it using your preferred method. You can also season the bread with herbs, spices, oil, cheese, or other ingredients before dehydrating it, depending on what you want to use the dehydrated bread for.

Breadcrumbs: You can use any non-oily bread, such as sourdough, rye, or homemade bread, to make breadcrumbs for baking or coating. You can slice the bread into **1/4 inch (6 mm)** slices or cubes, or pulse it in a food processor to make crumbs. Then, place them on dehydrator trays and dry them at **150°F (65°C)** for **1–3 hours**, until they are dry and crumbly. One pound

(454 g) of fresh bread will yield about **4 cups (240 g)** of breadcrumbs. Breadcrumbs have a crunchy texture and a mild flavor, and they can be used to add texture and flavor to dishes like meatballs, casseroles, or salads.

Croutons: You can also use non-oily bread to make croutons for soups, salads, or snacks. You can cube the bread to your desired size, and season it with herbs, spices, oil, or cheese if you like. Then, spread them on dehydrator trays and dry them at **150°F (65°C)** for **2–4 hours**, until they are crisp and golden. You can store them in an airtight container for 2–3 months, but check often for rancidity. One pound (454 g) of fresh bread will yield about **8 cups (400 g)** of croutons. Croutons have a crispy texture and a savory flavor, and they can be used to add crunch and taste to dishes like soups, salads, or stuffing.

Stuffing mix: You can use any bread you like to make stuffing mix for poultry, pork, or vegetables. You can cube the bread to your desired size, and season it with herbs, spices, onion, celery, or other ingredients if you like. Then, spread them on dehydrator trays and dry them at **150°F (65°C)** for **2–4 hours**, until they are dry and slightly browned. 1 pound (454 g) of fresh bread will yield about **8 cups (480 g)** of stuffing mix. Stuffing mix has a soft and moist texture and a rich flavor, and it can be used to fill and flavor dishes like turkey, chicken, or squash.

Cake: You can use any cake you like to make a dehydrated cake for desserts or snacks. You can slice the cake into **1/4 inch (6 mm)** slices or cubes, or crumble it into small pieces. Then, place them on dehydrator trays and dry them at **125°F (52°C)** for **4–6 hours**, until they are dry and brittle. One pound (454 g) of fresh cake will yield about 4 cups (240 g) of dehydrated cake. Dehydrated cake has a crunchy and crumbly texture and a sweet flavor, and it can be used to make desserts like pudding, parfait, or cheesecake.

Cheese

How to choose

Choosing quality cheese for dehydration is important, as it affects the taste, texture, and shelf life of the final product. Here are some tips to help you select the best cheese for your dehydrating project:

- Look for cheese that is hard or semi-hard, such as cheddar, Parmesan, Gouda, or Swiss. These cheeses have less moisture and will dry faster and more evenly than soft cheeses like brie, mozzarella, or cream cheese.

- Check the expiry date on the packaging. Cheese that is close to its expiration date may have more bacteria or mold growth, which could affect the quality and safety of the dehydrated cheese. Choose cheese that has a long shelf life and is fresh.

- Avoid cheese that has additives or preservatives, such as artificial colors, flavors, or stabilizers. These ingredients may interfere with the dehydrating process and reduce the nutritional value of the cheese. Look for cheese that is natural, organic, or made with simple ingredients.

- Taste the cheese before dehydrating it. The flavor of the cheese will intensify after dehydrating, so make sure you like how it tastes. You can also experiment with different types of cheese and mix and match them to create your blends.

Crumble cheese: Freeze a block of cheese and then crumble it into small pieces. Lay the cheese pieces directly on the rack in the dehydrator. Turn the dehydrator on and set the temperature to **130°F (54°C)**. Flip the cheese pieces over every three hours. Remove the cheese pieces from the dehydrator when they are fully dry, which may take **12 to 24 hours**. You will get about **1/4 pound (113 g)** of dried cheese from 1 pound (454 g) of raw cheese. The dried cheese will have a crunchy texture and a mild flavor. You can use it as a snack or sprinkle it on salads, soups, popcorn, etc.

Grate cheese: Grate cheese using a cheese grater or a food processor. Spread the cheese shreds evenly on a dehydrator tray lined with parchment paper or a fruit leather sheet. Set the dehydrator to **125°F (52°C)** and dry the cheese for **8 to 12 hours**, or until it is brittle and crumbly. You will get about **1/3 pound (150 g)** of dried cheese from 1 pound (454 g) of raw cheese. The dried cheese will have a powdery texture and a strong flavor. You can use it to make cheese sauces, dips, macaroni and cheese, etc.

Cube cheese: Cut cheese into small cubes, no more than **1/3 inch (0.8 cm)** thick. Place the cheese cubes on a dehydrator tray in a single layer, leaving some space between them. Set the dehydrator to **135°F (57°C)** and dry the cheese for **10 to 14 hours**, or until it is hard and dry. You will get about **1/2 pound (227 g)** of dried cheese from 1 pound (454 g) of raw cheese. The dried cheese will have a firm texture and a moderate flavor. You can use it as a snack or rehydrate it with hot water to make cheese cubes.

Slice cheese: Slice cheese thinly into small pieces, about **1/8 inch (0.3 cm)** thick. Place the cheese slices on a dehydrator tray in a single layer, making sure they are not touching each other. Set the dehydrator to **130-140°F (54-60°C)** and let the cheese dry for several hours, checking on it periodically. You will get about **2/3 pounds (300 g)** of dried cheese from 1 pound (454 g) of raw cheese. The dried cheese will have a chewy texture and a mild flavor. You can use it as a snack or add it to sandwiches, crackers, etc.

Melt cheese: Melt cheese in a saucepan over low heat, stirring constantly. Pour the melted cheese onto a dehydrator tray lined with parchment paper or a fruit leather sheet. Spread the cheese evenly with a spatula, making sure it is not too thin or too thick. Set the dehydrator to **145°F (63°C)** and dry the cheese for **6 to 8 hours**, or until it is dry and brittle. You will get about **3/4 pound (340 g)** of dried cheese from 1 pound (454 g) of raw cheese. The dried cheese will have a crispy texture and a strong flavor. You can use it to make cheese chips, crackers, or flakes.

Cheese powder: Use the recipe "Grate cheese" and then grind the cheese into a powder using a cheese grinder or a food processor.

Herbs

How to choose and prepare

When choosing herbs for dehydration, you should consider the type of herb, the moisture content, the freshness, and the intended use. Hardy herbs like rosemary, thyme, oregano, and sage have a low moisture content and retain their flavors well when dried. Fresh herbs that are bright and free of bruises or blemishes will give you the best results. You should harvest them in the morning after the dew has dried, but before the sun heats them and reduces their aromatic oils. You should also wash them thoroughly and pat them dry to remove any dirt or insects and discard any damaged or diseased leaves. Furthermore, you can experiment with different combinations of herbs to create your blends, such as Italian, Herbes de Provence, or Za'atar. You can also add other ingredients, such as garlic, lemon, or chili, to enhance the flavor and variety of your dried herbs.

You can use a dehydrator for nearly all herbs. Delicate herbs, such as chives, cilantro, and parsley, lose a lot of their flavor and aroma when dried. They are better preserved by freezing or using fresh. Here are some common steps for dehydrating herbs in a dehydrator:

- Arrange the herbs on the dehydrator trays: If you're using a tray that has large holes, line it with parchment paper or a mesh liner cut to the size of your tray. Leave space between the pieces to allow air to circulate. You can dry different herbs at the same time, as the flavors will not mix.

- Set the dehydrator temperature and time: Set the dehydrator to a low temperature, between 85°F to 105°F (29°C to 40°C), to preserve the color and flavor of the herbs. The drying time will vary depending on the type and moisture content of the herbs, but it usually ranges from 1 to 4 hours. Check the herbs periodically for dryness. They are done when they are crisp and crumble easily.

- Cool and store the dried herbs: Let the herbs cool completely before storing them.

50 herbs that dry well in a dehydrator

Short time (1 to 2 hours): These herbs have low moisture content and dry quickly. They include bay leaves, dill, marjoram, oregano, rosemary, sage, thyme, and lemon thyme.

Medium time (2 to 4 hours): These herbs have moderate moisture content and take a bit longer to dry. They include basil, cilantro, Italian parsley, mint, tarragon, lavender, savory, fennel, coriander, chamomile, lemon verbena, lemongrass, nettle, peppermint, spearmint, catnip, anise hyssop, bee balm, calendula, echinacea, feverfew, lemon balm, lovage, moringa, mullein, plantain, red clover, St. John's wort, stevia, and yarrow.

Long time (4 to 8 hours): These herbs have a high moisture content and take the longest to dry. They include chives, garlic, ginger, turmeric, horseradish, onion, celery, carrot, parsnip, cumin, and mustard.

Beans and Lentils

How to choose

Choose beans and lentils that are dry, firm, clean, and unshriveled. The color and shape of the beans and lentils should be uniform. Choose beans and lentils that cook quickly and easily, such as black beans, kidney beans, chickpeas, red lentils, and green lentils. Choose beans and lentils that are organic, non-GMO, and free of pesticides, additives, and preservatives, to ensure the quality and safety of your food. Choose canned beans and lentils if you want to save time and water, as they do not require pre-soaking and cook faster than dried beans and lentils. Canned beans and lentils also dehydrate and rehydrate better than home-cooked beans and lentils.

How to prepare and dehydrate

Soak the beans and lentils in water for 6 to 8 hours or overnight, then drain and rinse them well. Cook the beans and lentils in water or broth until they are soft and tender, then drain them again. Spread the beans and lentils on dehydrator trays in a single or thin layer, leaving some space between them for air circulation. Dehydrate the beans and lentils at 125°F (52°C) for 8 to 12 hours, or until they are hard and dry. They should not be soft or squishy.

Grains

How to choose

You can dehydrate many types of grains, such as wheat, corn, rice, oats, barley, quinoa, sorghum, spelled, and rye. Sprouted grains can also be dehydrated to preserve their nutrients and enzyme activity, but they need to be dehydrated at an even lower temperature, below 113°F (45°C). You need to check the condition of grains before dehydration to ensure they are fresh, clean, and free of insects, mold, or spoilage. You can do this by inspecting the grains visually, smelling them, and tasting a small sample. You should also rinse the grains well before cooking them, to remove any dust, dirt, or debris.

How to prepare

Cook your grains before dehydration to ensure they are safe and easy to rehydrate. Cooking can also improve the flavor, texture, and nutrition of the grains. The cooking time and method may vary depending on the type and size of the grains, but generally, you need to boil them in water or broth until they are tender. Then, you need to drain and fluff them with a fork before spreading them on dehydrator trays.

Wheat berries: Cook 1 pound (0.45 kg) of wheat berries in 4 cups (0.95 L) of boiling water for 45 minutes or until tender. Drain and spread on dehydrator trays in a single layer. Dehydrate at 130°F (54°C) for 8 to 10 hours, or until hard and dry. The grains are chewy, nutty, and brown, with a mild wheat flavor. They are good for making bread, cereal, or salads.

Quinoa: Rinse 1 pound (0.45 kg) of quinoa well and cook in 2 cups (473 ml) of water for 15 minutes or until fluffy. Fluff with a fork and spread on dehydrator trays in a thin layer. Dehydrate at 125°F (52°C) for 6 to 8 hours, or until crisp and dry. The grains are light, crunchy, and beige, with a slightly nutty flavor. They are great for making soups, stews, or casseroles.

Oats: Cook 1 pound (0.45 kg) of rolled oats in 4 cups (0.95 L) of water for 5 minutes, or until soft. Stir well and spread on dehydrator trays in a thin layer. Dehydrate at 130°F (54°C) for 6 to 8 hours, or until brittle and dry. The grains are flaky, crumbly, and pale, with a sweet and oatmeal flavor. They are perfect for making granola, cookies, or porridge.

Rice: Cook 1 pound (0.45 kg) of white rice in 2 cups (473 ml) of water for 20 minutes, or until tender. Fluff with a fork and spread on dehydrator trays in a single layer. Dehydrate at 125°F (52°C) for 6 to 8 hours, or until hard and dry. The grains are firm, smooth, and white, with a bland and starchy flavor. They are ideal for making fried rice, pilaf, or pudding.

Barley: Cook 1 pound (0.45 kg) of pearl barley in 3 cups (709 ml) of water for 40 minutes, or until soft. Drain and spread on dehydrator trays in a single layer. Dehydrate at 130°F (54°C) for 8 to 10 hours, or until hard and dry. The grains are chewy, plump, and tan, with a slightly malty flavor. They are wonderful for making risotto, salad, or soup.

Corn: Cook corn kernels in boiling water for a few minutes, then drain and spread on dehydrator trays in a single layer. Dehydrate at 125°F (52°C) for 6 to 8 hours, or until crisp and dry. The grains are sweet, crunchy, and yellow, with a corn flavor. They are great for making cornbread, muffins, or salsa.

Sorghum: Cook 1 pound (0.45 kg) of sorghum grains in 4 cups (946 ml) of boiling water for 45 minutes, or until tender. Drain and spread on dehydrator trays in a single layer. Dehydrate at 130°F (54°C) for 8 to 10 hours, or until hard and dry1. The grains are chewy, nutty, and red, with a mild sorghum flavor. They are great for making pilaf, salad, or porridge.

Spelled: Cook 1 pound (0.45 kg) of spelled grains in 3 cups (709 ml) of boiling water for 40 minutes, or until soft. Drain and spread on dehydrator trays in a single layer. Dehydrate at 130°F (54°C) for 8 to 10 hours, or until hard and dry1. The grains are plump, hearty, and brown, with a slightly sweet and nutty flavor. They are great for making bread, muffins, or cookies.

Rye: Cook 1 pound (0.45 kg) of rye grains in 4 cups (946 ml) of boiling water for 50 minutes, or until soft. Drain and spread on dehydrator trays in a single layer. Dehydrate at 130°F (54°C) for 8 to 10 hours, or until hard and dry1. The grains are chewy, earthy, and dark, with a rich and malty flavor. They are great for making crackers, pancakes, or beer.

Buckwheat: Rinse 1 pound (0.45 kg) of buckwheat groats well and cook in 2 cups (473 ml) of water for 15 minutes or until soft. Fluff with a fork and spread on dehydrator trays in a thin layer. Dehydrate at 125°F (52°C) for 6 to 8 hours, or until crisp and dry12. The grains are light, crunchy, and gray, with a slightly bitter and nutty flavor. They are great for making granola.

Sprouted grains:

Dehydrating sprouted grains is a way to preserve their nutrients and enzyme activity, as well as make them shelf-stable and ready for grinding into flour or use in other recipes. To dehydrate sprouted grains, you need to follow these general steps:

- Choose whole grains that are suitable for sprouting, such as wheat, barley, rye, spelled, quinoa, or buckwheat.
- Rinse the grains well and soak them in water for 8 to 12 hours, or until they swell and soften.
- Drain the grains and rinse them again, then transfer them to a sprouting jar, tray, or bag.
- Keep the grains moist and warm, but not wet or hot, and rinse them 2 to 3 times a day, until they sprout[12]. The sprouting time may vary depending on the type and freshness of the grains but usually takes 2 to 4 days.
- Drain the sprouted grains and spread them on dehydrator trays in a single or thin layer, leaving some space between them for air circulation.
- Dehydrate the sprouted grains at a low temperature, below 113°F (45°C), to preserve the enzyme activity. The dehydrating time may vary depending on the type and size of the grains but usually takes 12 to 24 hours.

Fruit leather

How to choose

Fruit leather is a delicious and healthy snack that can be made at home with a dehydrator. Fruit leather is essentially fruit puree that has been slowly dried to a thin, pliable sheet with the supple consistency of leather. You can use any fruit you like, or mix different fruits, to create your flavors. Some fruits that work well for fruit leather are:

- Berries - like strawberries, blueberries, raspberries, blackberries
- Stone fruits - e.g. apricots, plums, peaches
- Tropical fruits - like mangos and papaya

Other fruits - like apples, pears, kiwi, and grapes are also great fillers if you have some surplus strawberries or cherries. You can add sweeteners like honey or agave nectar, or spices like cinnamon or nutmeg, to enhance the flavor. The steps to make fruit leather are:

How to dehydrate

- Procure your fruit. You can use fresh or canned fruit, preferably ripe or overripe.
- Prepare your dehydrator trays. Lightly spray them with oil or use parchment paper to prevent sticking.
- Blend your fruit. You can add sweeteners like honey or agave nectar, or spices like cinnamon or nutmeg, to enhance the flavor.
- Pour your fruit puree onto the trays. Spread it evenly in a thin layer, about 1/8-inch thick.
- Turn on your dehydrator and set the temperature to 130°F (54°C).
- Dehydrate your fruit for at least six hours, or until it feels dry and leathery to the touch.
- Cool your fruit leather and peel it off the trays. Cut it into strips and roll it up with parchment paper.

Tips & Tricks

- Applesauce can be used as a filler or an extender for other fruits. It also decreases tartness and makes the leather smoother and more pliable.

- You can add sweeteners like honey or agave nectar, or spices like cinnamon or nutmeg, to enhance the flavor. The amount of sweetener is a personal preference, so you can adjust it to your liking.

- You can also add nuts, seeds, granola, or other crunchy ingredients to your fruit puree for some texture and extra nutrition.

- To prevent sticking, lightly spray your dehydrator trays with oil or use parchment paper. You can also use silicone mats or fruit roll sheets, if you have them.

- Spread your fruit puree evenly to a thin layer, about 1/8-inch thick, on the trays. If it is too thick, it will take longer to dry and may crack. If it is too thin, it may become brittle and hard to peel off.

- Set your dehydrator temperature to 130°F (54°C) and dehydrate your fruit for at least six hours, or until it feels dry and leathery to the touch. The drying time may vary depending on the type and moisture content of the fruit, the thickness of the puree, and the humidity of the environment.

- To test if your fruit leather is done, touch it with your finger. It should not feel sticky or tacky, and it should peel off easily from the tray. You can also bend it slightly and see if it cracks or tears. If it does, it needs more drying time.

- Once your fruit leather is done, let it cool completely before peeling it off the trays.

- The best time to cut or precut fruit leather is when it is fully dried and has a pliable texture. Cut it into strips or shapes and roll it up with parchment paper. You can use a pizza cutter or a knife to cut it into strips or shapes. You can also use scissors or cookie cutters to make fun shapes for kids.

- Store your fruit leather in an airtight container in a cool, dry place. It can last for several weeks or months, depending on the fruit and storage conditions. You can also freeze it for a longer shelf life.

Here are some common methods of pre-treating and how to use them:

Lemon juice or other citrus juices: These are natural sources of ascorbic acid, which is a type of vitamin C that acts as an antioxidant and prevents browning. You can use lemon, lime, orange, grapefruit, or pineapple juice to pre-treat your ingredients. To use this method, you need to dilute the juice with water in a ratio of 1:4 (one part juice to four parts water) and soak the ingredients for about 10 minutes. Then, drain and pat them dry before dehydrating. This method works well for fruits like apples, bananas, peaches, and pears. It can also add a tangy flavor to your dehydrated food.

Ascorbic acid: This is synthetic forms of vitamin C that have the same effect as citrus juices, but without the added flavor. You can buy ascorbic acid powder from a pharmacy or a grocery store. To use this method, you need to dissolve 2 teaspoons of ascorbic acid in one quart of water and soak the ingredients for about 10 minutes. Then, drain and pat them dry before dehydrating. This method works well for fruits and vegetables that are prone to browning.

Honey dip: This is a method of coating the ingredients with honey solution, which helps retain the moisture, flavor, and color of the dehydrated food. It can also make the food sweeter and softer. To use this method, you need to boil 1/2 cup of sugar in 1 1/2 cups of water and let it cool slightly. Then, stir in 2/3 cup of honey and soak the ingredients for about 3 minutes. Drain and place them on the dehydrator trays. This method works well for fruits like cranberries, cherries, and grapes.

- Arrange the ingredients in a single layer on the dehydrator trays. Leave some space between them for air circulation. Do not mix different types of ingredients on the same tray, as they may have different drying times and temperatures.

- Set the dehydrator to the appropriate temperature and time for the ingredients. Generally, fruits are dehydrated at 130°F to 140°F (54°C to 60°C) for 6 to 12 hours, and herbs and flowers are dehydrated at 95°F to 115°F (35°C to 46°C) for 2 to 4 hours. Check the ingredients periodically and rotate the trays if needed for even drying.

- - Store the dehydrated ingredients in airtight containers, such as glass jars, ziplock bags, or metal tins. Label the containers with the name and date of the ingredients. Keep them in a cool, dry, and dark place, away from direct sunlight and strong odors. Use them within 6 to 12 months for optimal freshness and flavor.

- - Experiment with different combinations and proportions of ingredients to create your own tea blends. You can also add pure teas, such as black, green, white, or oolong, to your blends for more variety and caffeine. To brew your tea, use 1 teaspoon of tea per 8 oz (230ml) of water. Adjust the water temperature and steeping time according to the type of tea you are using. Add sweeteners, milk, or lemon if desired. Enjoy your tea hot or cold.

Here are a few recipes of fruit leather for inspiration, if you want to try making your own fruit leather, you can use different fruits and flavors and experiment.

100 Fruit Leather Recipes

Apple and blueberry
Apple and cherry
Apple and cinnamon
Apple and cranberry
Apple and lemon
Apple and nutmeg
Apple and raspberry
Apricot and almond
Apricot and apple
Apricot and cherry
Apricot and peach
Apricot and plum
Banana and coconut
Banana and Nutella
Banana and peanut butter
Banana and strawberry
Blackberry and apple
Blackberry and lemon
Blackberry and orange
Blackberry and peach
Blackberry and pear
Blackberry and raspberry
Blueberry and banana
Blueberry and cherry
Blueberry and coconut
Blueberry and lemon
Blueberry and peach
Cantaloupe and honeydew
Cantaloupe and lime
Cantaloupe and strawberry
Carrot and apple
Cherry and almond
Cherry and lime

Cherry and peach
Cherry and vanilla
Coconut and pineapple
Cranberry and apple
Cranberry and lemon
Cranberry and orange
Cranberry and pear
Dragon fruit and banana
Dragon fruit and coconut
Dragon fruit and lime
Dragon fruit and raspberry
Grape and apple
Grape and lemon
Grape and pear
Grape and raspberry
Kiwi and lime
Kiwi and mango
Kiwi and pineapple
Kiwi and strawberry
Mango and banana
Mango and coconut
Mango and lime
Mango and orange
Mango and passion fruit
Mango and pineapple
Mango and strawberry
Peach and apricot
Peach and banana
Peach and blueberry
Peach and ginger
Peach and lemon
Peach and mango
Peach and nectarine
Peach and orange

Peach and plum
Peach and raspberry
Pear and blueberry
Pear and ginger
Pear and lemon
Pear and vanilla
Pineapple and banana
Pineapple and coconut
Pineapple and lime
Plum and apricot
Plum and blackberry
Plum and cherry
Plum and peach
Plum and raspberry
Pumpkin and spice
Raspberry and chocolate
Raspberry and lemon
Raspberry and orange
Raspberry and peach
Rhubarb and apple
Rhubarb and cherry
Rhubarb and peach
Rhubarb and strawberry
Starfruit and banana
Starfruit and ginger
Starfruit and kiwi
Starfruit and mango
Starfruit and pineapple
Strawberry and banana
Strawberry and beet
Strawberry and kiwi
Strawberry and orange
Strawberry and rhubarb
Watermelon and mint

Vegetable leather

How to choose

Choose vegetables that have a mild or sweet flavor, such as carrots, pumpkin, sweet potatoes, beets, tomatoes, spinach, zucchini, kale, broccoli, cauliflower, peas, corn, cucumbers, celery, parsnips, squash, bell peppers, eggplant, mushrooms, or asparagus.

How to prepare

- Cook the vegetables until soft and puree them in a blender or food processor. You can add water if needed to make a smooth puree.
- Add spices, herbs, or sweeteners to the puree to enhance the flavor. You can use salt, pepper, garlic, onion, basil, oregano, thyme, rosemary, curry, cumin, paprika, cinnamon, nutmeg, ginger, cloves, honey, maple syrup, agave nectar, or lemon juice, depending on the type of vegetable and your preference.
- Taste the puree and adjust the seasoning as needed. Remember that the flavor will intensify as the puree dries, so use them sparingly.
- You can also mix different vegetables together to create your own combinations or add fruits, nuts, seeds, cheese, or other ingredients to the puree for more variety and nutrition.

How to dehydrate

- Spread the puree evenly on a baking sheet or a dehydrator tray lined with parchment paper or a silicone mat. The thickness should be about 1/8 inch.
- Dry the puree in an oven or a dehydrator at 140°F (60°C) for 6 to 10 hours, or until it is dry and leathery. The drying time may vary depending on the moisture content of the puree and the humidity of the environment.
- Peel the vegetable leather off the liner and cut it into strips or shapes. You can also roll it up with parchment paper for easy storage and consumption.

50 Vegetable Leather Recipes

Asparagus and cheese

Asparagus and lemon

Asparagus and Parmesan

Beet and apple

Beet and orange

Beet and strawberry

Bell pepper and cheese

Bell pepper and eggplant

Bell pepper and garlic

Bell pepper and onion

Bell pepper and tomato

Broccoli and cheddar

Carrot and apple

Carrot and ginger

Carrot and pineapple

Carrot and pumpkin

Cauliflower and cheese

Cauliflower and curry

Cauliflower and garlic

Celery and apple

Celery and cheese

Celery and peanut butter

Corn and honey

Cucumber and lime

Cucumber and mint

Eggplant and cheese

Eggplant and Parmesan

Eggplant and tomato

Kale and coconut

Kale and pineapple

Mushroom and cheese

Mushroom and rosemary

Mushroom and thyme

Parsnip and honey

Parsnip and pear

Pea and mint

Pumpkin and apple

Pumpkin and cranberry

Pumpkin and spice

Spinach and cheese

Spinach and garlic

Squash and ginger

Squash and nutmeg

Sweet potato and cinnamon

Sweet potato and coconut

Tomato and basil

Tomato and cheese

Tomato and oregano

Zucchini and lemon

Zucchini and mint

Tea blends

Tea is one of the most popular and versatile beverages in the world. It can be enjoyed hot or cold, sweet, or bitter, plain or flavored. Tea can also have various health benefits, such as antioxidants, anti-inflammatory, and calming effects. But did you know that you can make your own tea blends at home using a dehydrator?

You can use a dehydrator to dry fruits, herbs, flowers, and spices that you can then use to create your own tea blends. You can also use store-bought or homegrown dried ingredients for this purpose.

Making your own tea blends with a dehydrator is easy, fun, and rewarding. You can save money, experiment with different combinations, and ensure the quality and freshness of your tea. You can also customize your tea to suit your taste preferences and health needs. You can make tea blends that are fruity, floral, herbal, spicy, or any combination you like. You can also add pure teas, such as black, green, white, or oolong, to your blends for more variety and caffeine.

In this chapter, you will learn how to make tea with a dehydrator, including how to choose, prepare, dry, store, and brew your ingredients. You will also find some examples of tea blends that you can try, or use as inspiration to create your own. Whether you are a tea lover, a dehydrator enthusiast, or both, you will find this chapter useful and enjoyable.

Custom blends for your taste preferences

Making a custom tea blend is a fun and creative way to experiment with different flavors and ingredients. You can use pure teas, dried herbs, flowers, fruits, spices, and even flavorings or oils to create your unique blends. Here are some general steps and tips for making your tea blends:

- Choose a base ingredient. This is usually a pure tea (such as black, green, white, oolong, or Pu'erh) or a dried herb (such as peppermint, chamomile, or rooibos) that will provide the main flavor and body of your blend. You can use one or more base ingredients, depending on your preference. The base ingredient should make up about 50% to 80% of your blend.

- Choose a supporting ingredient. This is an ingredient that will complement and enhance the flavor of your base ingredient. It can be another tea, herb, flower, fruit, spice, or flavoring. For example, if your base ingredient is black tea, you can add dried orange peel, vanilla beans, or bergamot oil to create different variations of Earl Grey tea. The supporting ingredient should make up about 10% to 40% of your blend.

- Choose an accent ingredient. This is an ingredient that will add a pop of flavor, aroma, or color to your blend. It can be a flower, fruit, spice, or flavoring that will give your blend a distinctive character. For example, if your base ingredient is green tea and your supporting ingredient is dried peach slices, you can add lavender buds, ginger pieces, or honeybush tea to create different variations of peach tea. The accent ingredient should make up about 5% to 15% of your blend.

- Mix and store your blend. Combine your ingredients in a glass jar and shake well to mix. Label your jar with the name and date of your blend. Store your blend in a cool, dry, and dark place, away from direct sunlight and strong odors. Use your blend within 6 to 12 months for optimal freshness and flavor.

- Brew and enjoy your blend. To brew your blend, use 1 teaspoon of tea per 8 oz of water. Adjust the water temperature and steeping time according to the type of tea you are using. For example, use boiling water and steep for 3 to 5 minutes for black tea, and use hot water and steep for 2 to 3 minutes for green tea. You can also experiment with different ratios and steeping times to find your preferred strength and taste. Add sweeteners, milk, or lemon if desired. Enjoy your custom tea blend hot or cold.

Here are some tips and tricks for making tea in a dehydrator:

- Choose fresh and organic ingredients whenever possible. Wash them well and pat them dry before dehydrating.

- Cut the ingredients into uniform pieces for even drying. Remove any stems, pits, or cores that may affect the taste or texture of the tea.

- Pre-treat the ingredients to prevent browning and enhance the flavor. You can use lemon juice, ascorbic acid, honey, or other natural preservatives to coat the ingredients before dehydrating.

Popular blends

1. Rose, Citrus, Berry, and Apple Tea

Ingredients: 1 ½ lbs (680 g) each of fresh apples, oranges, and strawberries; 1 ½ cups (90 g) of dried orange slices; 1 ½ cups (90 g) of dried apple slices; 1 ½ cups (90 g) of dried strawberry slices; 1 ½ cups (30 g) of dried rose petals; 2 cups (40 g) of white tea; ½ cup (10 g) of dried herbs (optional, such as wormwood, or mint).

Cut: Slice the apples and oranges into ¼ inch (0.6 cm) thick rings. Hull and slice the strawberries into ¼ inch (0.6 cm) thick pieces.

Temperature and time: Preheat the dehydrator to 135°F (57°C). Blanch the fruit slices in boiling water for 30 seconds, then run under cold water and drain. Soak the fruit slices in a solution of 2 ½ tablespoons (37 g) of ascorbic acid crystals and one quart (0.95 L) of chilled water for 10 minutes, then drain. Arrange the fruit slices in a single layer on the dehydrator trays. Dehydrate for 6 to 12 hours, or until dry and leathery. Store in an airtight container.

Yield: About 4 ½ cups (270 g) of dried fruit slices.

Taste, color, and texture: The tea has a sweet, fruity, and floral flavor, with a hint of citrus and herbs. The color is a pale yellow with specks of red, orange, green, and pink. The texture is smooth and soothing.

Use: To brew the tea, use 1 tablespoon (5 g) of the tea blend per 8 oz (240 ml) of water. Steep for 3 to 5 minutes, or longer for a stronger flavor. Enjoy hot or cold.

2. Lemon, Ginger, and Turmeric Tea

Ingredients: 2 lemons; 4 oz (113 g) of fresh ginger root; 2 oz (57 g) of fresh turmeric root; 2 cups (40 g) of green tea.

Cut: Peel and slice the lemons into ¼ inch (0.6 cm) thick rings. Peel and slice the ginger and turmeric into ⅛ inch (0.3 cm) thick pieces.

Temperature and time: Preheat the dehydrator to 135°F (57°C). Arrange the lemon, ginger, and turmeric slices in a single layer on the dehydrator trays. Dehydrate for 6 to 8 hours, or until dry and crisp. Store in an airtight container.

Yield: About 2 cups (120 g) of dried lemon, ginger, and turmeric slices.

Taste, color, and texture: The tea has a tangy, spicy, and earthy flavor, with a refreshing and warming effect. The color is a bright yellow with hints of orange and brown. The texture is crisp and crunchy.

Use: To brew the tea, use 1 tablespoon (5 g) of the tea blend per 8 oz (240 ml) of water. Steep for 3 to 5 minutes, or longer for a stronger flavor. Add honey or sugar to sweeten if desired. Enjoy hot or cold.

3. Lavender, Chamomile, and Mint Tea

Ingredients: 1 cup (10 g) of dried lavender buds; 1 cup (10 g) of dried chamomile flowers; 1 cup (10 g) of dried mint leaves; 2 cups (40 g) of black tea.

Cut: No cutting required.

Temperature and time: No dehydrating required. You can use store-bought or homegrown dried herbs and flowers for this recipe. Store in an airtight container.

Yield: About 4 cups (80 g) of dried tea blend.

Taste, color, and texture: The tea has a floral, herbal, and minty flavor, with a calming and relaxing effect. The color is a light brown with specks of purple, yellow, and green. The texture is soft and fluffy.

Use: To brew the tea, use 1 tablespoon (5 g) of the tea blend per 8 oz (240 ml) of water. Steep for 3 to 5 minutes, or longer for a stronger flavor. Add honey or sugar to sweeten if desired. Enjoy hot or cold.

4. Peach, Vanilla, and Honeybush Tea

Ingredients: 2 cups (40 g) of honeybush tea; 1 cup (20 g) of dried peach slices; 1/4 cup (5 g) of dried vanilla beans; 2 tablespoons (30 g) of honey.

Cut: Cut the dried peach slices into small pieces. Cut the dried vanilla beans into 1/4 inch (0.6 cm) segments.

Temperature and time: No dehydrating required. You can use store-bought or home-dried peach slices and vanilla beans for this recipe. Store in an airtight container.

Yield: About 3 cups (65 g) of dried tea blend.

Taste, color, and texture: The tea has a sweet, fruity, and creamy flavor, with a soothing and comforting effect. The color is a golden brown with specks of yellow and black. The texture is soft and chewy.

Use: To brew the tea, use 1 tablespoon (5 g) of the tea blend per 8 oz (240 ml) of water. Steep for 5 to 7 minutes, or longer for a stronger flavor. Add more honey to sweeten if desired. Enjoy hot or cold.

5. Cranberry, Hibiscus, and Rooibos Tea

Ingredients: 2 cups (40 g) of rooibos tea; 1 cup (20 g) of dried cranberries; 1/2 cup (10 g) of dried hibiscus flowers; 1/4 cup (5 g) of dried orange peel.

Cut: Cut the dried cranberries into small pieces. Cut the dried orange peel into thin strips.

Temperature and time: No dehydrating required. You can use store-bought or home-dried cranberries, hibiscus flowers, and orange peel for this recipe. Store in an airtight container.

Yield: About 3 1/2 cups (75 g) of dried tea blend.

Taste, color, and texture: The tea has a tart, tangy, and refreshing flavor, with a cleansing and energizing effect. The color is a deep red with hints of orange and green. The texture is crisp and crunchy.

Use: To brew the tea, use 1 tablespoon (5 g) of the tea blend per 8 oz (240 ml) of water. Steep for 5 to 7 minutes, or longer for a stronger flavor. Add sugar or honey to sweeten if desired. Enjoy hot or cold.

6. Coconut, Chocolate, and Black Tea

Ingredients: 2 cups (40 g) of black tea; 1 cup (20 g) of shredded coconut; 1/2 cup (10 g) of cocoa nibs; 1/4 cup (5 g) of chocolate chips.

Cut: No cutting required.

Temperature and time: No dehydrating required. You can use store-bought or home-made shredded coconut, cocoa nibs, and chocolate chips for this recipe. Store in an airtight container.

Yield: About 3 1/2 cups (75 g) of dried tea blend.

Taste, color, and texture: The tea has a rich, decadent, and indulgent flavor, with a satisfying and stimulating effect. The color is a dark brown with specks of white and black. The texture is smooth and melty.

Use: To brew the tea, use 1 tablespoon (5 g) of the tea blend per 8 oz (240 ml) of water. Steep for 3 to 5 minutes, or longer for a stronger flavor. Add milk or cream to enhance the flavor if desired. Enjoy hot or cold.

7. Apple, Cinnamon, and Rooibos Tea

Ingredients: 2 cups (40 g) of rooibos tea; 1 cup (20 g) of dried apple slices; 1/4 cup (5 g) of cinnamon sticks; 2 tablespoons (30 g) of brown sugar.

Cut: Cut the dried apple slices into small pieces. Break the cinnamon sticks into 1/2 inch (1.3 cm) segments.

Temperature and time: No dehydrating required. You can use store-bought or home-dried apple slices and cinnamon sticks for this recipe. Store in an airtight container.

Yield: About 3 cups (65 g) of dried tea blend.

Taste, color, and texture: The tea has a cozy, sweet, and spicy flavor, with a soothing and warming effect. The color is a reddish brown with specks of yellow and brown. The texture is soft and chewy.

Use: To brew the tea, use 1 tablespoon (5 g) of the tea blend per 8 oz (240 ml) of water. Steep for 5 to 7 minutes, or longer for a stronger flavor. Add more sugar to sweeten if desired. Enjoy hot or cold.

8. Pineapple, Coconut, and Green Tea

Ingredients: 2 cups (40 g) of green tea; 1 cup (20 g) of dried pineapple chunks; 1/2 cup (10 g) of shredded coconut; 1/4 cup (5 g) of coconut flakes.

Cut: Cut the dried pineapple chunks into small pieces. No cutting required for the shredded coconut and coconut flakes.

Temperature and time: No dehydrating required. You can use store-bought or home-dried pineapple chunks, shredded coconut, and coconut flakes for this recipe. Store in an airtight container.

Yield: About 3 1/2 cups (75 g) of dried tea blend.

Taste, color, and texture: The tea has a tropical, fruity, and creamy flavor, with a refreshing and hydrating effect. The color is a light green with hints of yellow and white. The texture is crisp and crunchy.

Use: To brew the tea, use 1 tablespoon (5 g) of the tea blend per 8 oz (240 ml) of water. Steep for 2 to 3 minutes, or longer for a stronger flavor. Add honey or sugar to sweeten if desired. Enjoy hot or cold.

9. Ginger, Lemon, and White Tea

Ingredients: 2 cups (40 g) of white tea; 1 cup (20 g) of dried ginger slices; 1/4 cup (5 g) of dried lemon peel; 2 tablespoons (30 g) of honey.
Cut: Cut the dried ginger slices into small pieces. Cut the dried lemon peel into thin strips.
Temperature and time: No dehydrating required. You can use store-bought or home-dried ginger slices and lemon peel for this recipe. Store in an airtight container.
Yield: About 3 cups (65 g) of dried tea blend.
Taste, color, and texture: The tea has a zesty, spicy, and invigorating flavor, with a cleansing and energizing effect. The color is a pale yellow with hints of orange and brown. The texture is crisp and crunchy.
Use: To brew the tea, use 1 tablespoon (5 g) of the tea blend per 8 oz (240 ml) of water. Steep for 2 to 3 minutes, or longer for a stronger flavor. Add more honey to sweeten if desired. Enjoy hot or cold.

10. Mango, Passion Fruit, and Oolong Tea

Ingredients: 2 cups (40 g) of oolong tea; 1 cup (20 g) of dried mango slices; 1/2 cup (10 g) of dried passion fruit pulp; 1/4 cup (5 g) of dried marigold petals.

Cut: Cut the dried mango slices into small pieces. Cut the dried passion fruit pulp into thin strips.

Temperature and time: No dehydrating required. You can use store-bought or home-dried mango slices, passion fruit pulp, and marigold petals for this recipe. Store in an airtight container.

Yield: About 3 1/2 cups (75 g) of dried tea blend.

Taste, color, and texture: The tea has a tropical, sweet, and tangy flavor, with a refreshing and hydrating effect. The color is a bright yellow with hints of orange and green.

se: To brew the tea, use 1 tablespoon (5 g) of the tea blend per 8 oz (240 ml) of water. Steep for 3 to 5 minutes, or longer for a stronger flavor. Add honey or sugar to sweeten if desired. Enjoy hot or cold.

Dehydrated food for Pets

If you are looking for a way to feed your pets with high-quality, natural, and delicious food, you might want to consider dehydrated food. The dehydration process preserves the nutritional value, flavor, and aroma of the ingredients, while also extending their shelf life and making them easy to store and transport.

Dehydrated food is similar to raw food but without the risk of bacteria or spoilage. It is also different from dry food, which is highly processed and often contains artificial preservatives, fillers, and additives. Dehydrated food is made with real food ingredients, such as meat, fruits, vegetables, and grains, which are cooked at low temperatures to retain their natural enzymes, vitamins, and minerals.

Dehydrated food is suitable for pets of all ages, breeds, and sizes. It can provide a balanced and complete diet for your pets, as well as a variety of flavors and textures to suit their preferences and needs. Dehydrated food is also easy to prepare, as you only need to add water to rehydrate it before feeding. You can also customize it by adding fresh ingredients or supplements to create your own recipes.

In this book, you will find some tips and tricks on how to make your own dehydrated food at home, using a dehydrator. You will discover some of the best dehydrated food recipes for dogs, cats, and small animals, such as mice, hamsters, and guinea pigs. You will also learn how to store, serve, and transition your pets to dehydrated food, as well as how to avoid some common pitfalls and mistakes.

Whether you are new to dehydrated food or already a fan, this book will help you make informed and confident choices for your pets' health and happiness. Dehydrated food is not only a healthy and convenient option, but also a fun and rewarding way to bond with your pets and show them your love and care. So, what are you waiting for? Let's get started!

Choose the ingredients that you want to use, such as meat, fruits, or vegetables. Make sure they are safe and healthy for your pets.

Mice, Hamsters & Guinea Pigs

There are many possible food blends and treats that you can prepare for your Mice, Hamsters & Guinea Pigs in a dehydrator, using a variety of ingredients that are safe and healthy for them. Here are some examples, but you can also experiment with your own recipes, as long as you follow the general guidelines for feeding Mice, Hamsters & Guinea Pigs.

Food blends that are safe and healthy for your pets are:

Fruits: You can dehydrate fruits like apples, bananas, strawberries, blueberries, and cranberries. Fruits are rich in vitamin C, antioxidants, and fiber, and can help boost your pets' immune system and digestion. Dehydrate them at 135°F (57°C) for 6 to 10 hours, until leathery or crisp.

Vegetables: You can dehydrate vegetables like carrots, sweet potatoes, beets, parsnips, turnips, broccoli, and kale. Vegetables are high in vitamin A, beta-carotene, iron, calcium, and fiber, and can help improve your pets' vision, blood circulation, and skin health. Dehydrate them at 125°F to 155°F (52°C to 68°C) for 4 to 8 hours, until crisp or chewy.

Grains: You can dehydrate grains like oats, barley, quinoa, and rice. Grains are a good source of carbohydrates, protein, and fiber for your pets, and can help lower their cholesterol and blood sugar levels. Dehydrate them at 145°F (63°C) for 4 to 6 hours, until crunchy and golden.

Meat: You can dehydrate meat like chicken, beef, turkey, and salmon. Meat is a lean and tasty protein that provides your pets with iron, zinc, and amino acids. Dehydrate it at 155°F (68°C) for 6 to 8 hours, until hard and brittle. Remember to put it in the oven for 10 minutes at 150°C to kill any pathogens.

Keep in mind that mice, hamsters, and guinea pigs have different dietary preferences:

Mice are omnivores, so they need both meat and vegetables in their diet. They can eat a variety of fruits, vegetables, seeds, nuts, and even insects as treats, as long as they are given in moderation and follow some general guidelines.

Hamsters are also omnivores, but they have different nutritional requirements than mice. They need more protein and fat, and less sugar and starch, in their diet. They can eat some fruits, vegetables, seeds, nuts, and insects as treats, but they should avoid foods that are high in water, sugar, or acid, such as citrus fruits, grapes, and tomatoes.

Guinea pigs are herbivores, so they need mostly plant-based foods in their diet4. They can eat some fruits, vegetables, herbs, and flowers as treats, but they should limit their intake of sugary or starchy foods, such as bananas, corn, and potatoes. They also need a lot of vitamin C, which they can get from foods like bell peppers, broccoli, and parsley.

Treats

Limit the amount and frequency of treats, as they should not make up more than 10% of your pet's diet.

Carrots: Carrots are a favorite mouse and hamster food that helps keep their teeth short and healthy. Carrots are a favorite treat for many guinea pigs, but they should be given sparingly because of their high sugar content. You can dehydrate the carrots with or without the greens, but make sure to remove the tops. Cut the carrots into thin slices and dry them at 125°F (52°C) for about 6 hours, or until crisp.

Cucumber: Cucumber is a refreshing and hydrating treat for guinea pigs, especially in hot weather. It has vitamin C, vitamin K, and potassium, but it also has a lot of water, so it should be given sparingly. You can dehydrate the cucumber with or without the peel and the seeds, but make sure to wash it well. Cut it into thin slices and dry it at 125°F (52°C) for about 4 hours, or until crisp.

Apples: Apples are rich in iron, vitamin C, calcium, and vitamin K, but they also contain a lot of sugar. You can cut out a small cube of apple (without seeds) and dehydrate it for your pet. You can dehydrate any variety of apples, but make sure to remove the core and the seeds, as they are toxic. Don't remove the peel, as it has fiber and vitamins. Dry them at 135°F (57°C) for about 8 hours, or until leathery.

Celery: Celery is a low-calorie vegetable that can add some hydration and crunch to your mouse's diet. You can wash, cut, and dehydrate celery for your mouse, but make sure to chop it finely to avoid choking hazards. Dry them at 125°F (52°C) for about 8 hours, or until brittle.

Banana chips: Bananas are a sweet and nutritious treat for mice, but they can spoil quickly. It has potassium, magnesium, and vitamin B6, but it also has a lot of sugar and starch, so it should be given sparingly Just give a small piece once a week. You can dehydrate the banana with or without the peel, but make sure to peel it before feeding it to your guinea pigs. You can slice and dehydrate bananas to make banana chips that last longer and are easier to store. Dry them at 135°F (57°C) for about 8   or until crisp.

Pumpkin seeds: Pumpkin seeds are a good source of protein, fat, and minerals for mice. You can roast and dehydrate pumpkin seeds for your mouse, but make sure to remove the shell and salt. Give only one or two seeds per week, as they are high in fat2. Dry them at 125°F (52°C) for about 6 hours, or until crisp.

Bell peppers: Bell peppers are rich in vitamin C, which small pets need to prevent scurvy. You can dehydrate any color of bell pepper, but make sure to remove the seeds first. Cut the peppers into thin slices and dry them at 125°F (52°C) for about 6 hours, or until crisp.

Broccoli: Broccoli is another good source of vitamin C and fiber for mice. You can dehydrate the leaves and stems, but not the florets, as they may cause gas. Chop the broccoli into small pieces and dry them at 125°F (52°C) for about 8 hours, or until brittle.

Brussels sprouts: Brussels sprouts are low in calories and high in antioxidants for small pets. You can dehydrate them whole or cut them in half, depending on their size. Dry them at 125°F (52°C) for about 10 or until hard.

Parsnip: Parsnip is a root vegetable that small pets enjoy as an occasional treat. It has a sweet and nutty flavor and contains vitamin C, potassium, and folate. Peel and slice the parsnip and dry it at 125°F (52°C) for about 6 hours or until crisp.

Zucchini: Zucchini is a summer squash that mice, guinea pigs and hamster can eat in moderation. You can dehydrate it with or without the peel, but make sure to wash it well. Cut it into thin slices and dry it at 125°F (52°C) for about 5 hours, or until crisp.

Cabbage: Cabbage is a leafy green vegetable that guinea pigs can eat occasionally. It has vitamin C, vitamin K, and calcium, but it can also cause gas and bloating. You can dehydrate any type of cabbage, but avoid the red or purple varieties, as they may stain your dehydrator. Cut the cabbage into small pieces and dry it at 125°F (52°C) for about 8 hours, or until crisp.

Strawberry: which are delicious, juicy, and crisp, and provide vitamin C, antioxidants, and fiber for your pet. Dehydrate them at 135°F (57°C) for 8 to 10 hours, until dry and crisp.

Kale chips: which are mild, slightly bitter, and brittle, and provide vitamin K, calcium, iron, and antioxidants for your pet. Dehydrate them at 125°F (52°C) for 2 to 4 hours, until crisp.

Dried egg flakes: which are a complete protein that contain all the essential amino acids that your pet need (don't give it to guinea pigs), as well as calcium, phosphorus, and selenium. Dehydrate them at 145°F (63°C) for 6 to 8 hours, until dry and flaky.

Dried chicken jerky: which is a lean and tasty meat that provides your pet (don't give it to guinea pigs) with protein, iron, and zinc. Dehydrate it at 155°F (68°C) for 6 to 8 hours, until hard and brittle. Remember to put it in the oven for 10 minutes at 150°C to kill any pathogens.

Dried cheese cubes: which are a good source of protein and calcium for your pet (don't give it to guinea pigs), and can help strengthen their bones and teeth. Dehydrate them at 145°F (63°C) for 4 to 6 hours, until dry and hard.

Reptile & Fish

Dehydrating some vegetables and animal foods can be a good way to preserve some ingredients and save money. However, a complete diet for reptiles or fish requires a balance of protein, carbohydrates, fats, fiber, vitamins, and minerals. Dehydrating food may alter or reduce some of these nutrients, especially if the food is not prepared or stored properly. Therefore, make sure that your reptile or fish gets all the nutrients they need from their homemade food, and supplement their diet with other foods or products.

For reptiles

If you are growing crickets for reptiles, you can dehydrate them. These are high in protein and can be dusted with calcium powder for extra nutrition. Place the insects into the boiling liquid for about two minutes. Drain the crickets and place them in a container in your refrigerator to cool. Once cooled, spread the crickets onto a sheet in your dehydrator. To dehydrate insects, you can use a temperature of 145°F (62°C) for about 10 hours, or until they are completely dry but not overly crunchy. You can also dehydrate vegetables and fruits such as collard greens, carrot tops, lettuce, escarole, cabbage, broccoli, kale, cauliflower, Brussels sprouts, apple, banana, and mango. These are rich in vitamins and minerals and can provide variety to your reptile's diet. To dehydrate vegetables and fruits, you can use a temperature of 125°F-135°F (52°C-57°C) for about 8-12 hours, or until they are leathery and crisp. Avoid citrus fruits, lettuce, spinach, and avocado, as they can cause health problems for some reptiles.

For fish

There are different ways to preserve dry food for your fish, depending on the type of fish you have and the ingredients you want to use. Some common methods are drying fresh fish and blend it with dried vegetables.

To dehydrate fish for your fish:

- First, you need to choose a lean fish, such as cod, haddock, or tilapia. Fatty fish will spoil faster and may not dry well. You also need to use fresh fish, not frozen, to ensure the best quality.

- Next, you need to clean, gut, and skin your fish. You can also remove the bones, or leave them in if you want to add some extra calcium to your fish food.

- Then, you need to slice your fish into thin strips or pieces, about 1/4 inch (6mm) thick. You can also cut some slits in the flesh to help the drying process.

- Next, you need to rinse your fish and pat it dry with paper towels. Then, you need to arrange your fish on the dehydrator trays, leaving some space between them for air circulation.

- Finally, you need to set your dehydrator to a low temperature, around 95°F (35°C), and let it run for several hours until your fish is completely dry and brittle. You can check the progress by breaking a piece and seeing if there is any moisture inside.

Once your fish is dry, you can store it in an airtight container, in a cool and dark place, for up to six months. You can also grind it into a powder and mix it with other ingredients, such as dried vegetables, or grains, to make a balanced fish food. You can feed your fish by soaking some of the dry food in water for a few minutes, or by sprinkling it on the surface of the water.

To dehydrate vegetables for your fish:

- Choose fresh and organic vegetables that are suitable for your fish species, such as broccoli, zucchini, lettuce, or peas.

- Wash and dry the vegetables thoroughly to remove any dirt or pesticides.

- Cut the vegetables into thin slices or small pieces, depending on the size of your fish.

- Blanch or steam the vegetables for a few minutes to soften them and preserve their color and nutrients.
- Drain and pat the vegetables dry with paper towels.
- Arrange the vegetables on dehydrator trays, leaving some space between them for air circulation.
- Set the dehydrator to a low temperature, around 95°F (35°C), and let it run for several hours, until the vegetables are completely dry and brittle.
- Store the dehydrated vegetables in an airtight container, in a cool and dark place, for up to six months.

You can also grind the dehydrated vegetables into a powder and mix them with other ingredients, such as dried fish, fruits, or grains, to make a balanced fish food.

You can also experiment with different combinations of plant and animal matter to suit your reptile's and fish's dietary needs. However, you should always research the specific requirements of your pet species before feeding them homemade food, as some ingredients may be harmful or unsuitable for them. You should also introduce new foods gradually and monitor your pet's health and behavior.

Dogs

Dehydrated food and treats for dogs can be made from various ingredients, such as meat, fish, fruits, vegetables, and cheese. You can use a dehydrator, an oven, or even the sun to dehydrate food for your dog. Dehydrating food for your dog can be fun, easy, and economical, as you can use leftovers, scraps, or seasonal produce to make tasty treats for your furry friend.

Dehydrated food and treats for dogs can provide many benefits, such as:

- They can be used as a snack, a training reward, a supplement, or a meal topper for your dog.
- They can help improve your dog's dental health, as chewing on dehydrated treats can scrape off plaque and tartar from their teeth.
- They can help satisfy your dog's natural chewing instinct, as dehydrated treats can be chewy, crunchy, or crispy, depending on how long you dry them.
- They can help prevent food waste, as you can use food that would otherwise go bad or be thrown away to make dehydrated treats for your dog.
- They can help you control what your dog eats, as you can choose the ingredients and avoid any additives, preservatives, or allergens that may harm your dog.

Dehydrated food and treats for dogs are a great way to show your love and care for your dog, as you can make them with your own hands and customize them to your dog's preferences and needs. You can also experiment with different flavors, textures, and shapes to make dehydrated treats that your dog will enjoy. Dehydrated food and treats for dogs are a simple and natural way to feed your dog and keep them happy and healthy.

The shelf life of dehydrated dog food and treats depends on several factors, such as the ingredients and the storage conditions. In general, dehydrated dog food and treats can last from a few weeks to several months, depending on how they are stored.

To store dehydrated dog food and treats properly, you should follow these tips:

- Store them in an airtight container to prevent moisture and air from getting in.
- Store them in a cool, dark, and dry place, such as a pantry or a cupboard.
- Refrigerate or freeze them to extend their shelf life, but make sure to label the container with the date of storage and thaw them before feeding them to your dog.
- Avoid storing them in direct sunlight or in a warm area, as it can cause them to spoil faster.
- Check them regularly for signs of spoilage, such as a change in color, texture, or smell, and discard them if they are moldy, rancid, or stale.

There are some things that you should avoid
when making dog and cat treats in a dehydrator, such as:

- Ingredients that are toxic, allergenic, or low in nutritional value for dogs, such as chocolate, grapes, onions, garlic, corn, wheat, soy, xylitol, artificial colors, flavors, or preservatives, etc.
- Excessive salt, sugar, or fat, which can cause dehydration, obesity, high blood pressure, kidney damage, or pancreatitis in pets.
- Bones, seeds, pits, or cores, which can pose a choking hazard or cause intestinal blockage or perforation in pets.
- Uneven or too thick slices, which can cause inconsistent drying or spoilage in pets.

Dehydrated main food

Dehydrated food can be a good option for your dog's daily diet, as it can provide many benefits such as longer shelf life, fewer preservatives, and higher nutritional value. However, not all dehydrated food is suitable for your dog, and you need to consider some factors such as the quality and variety of the ingredients, the dehydration process and equipment, and your dog's age, size, activity level, and health condition.

Here are some dehydrated foods that are suitable for your dog's main food:

- **Dehydrated meat**: Meat is the main source of protein for your dog, and it can be dehydrated from various sources such as chicken, beef, lamb, turkey, pork, venison, etc. You can cut the meat into thin slices and dehydrate it at **145°F (63°C)** for **3 to 12 hours**, depending on the thickness and desired texture. You can also season the meat with salt, pepper, and herbs if you like, but avoid spices that may irritate your dog's stomach. One pound (0.45 kg) of raw meat will yield about **4 ounces (113 g)** of dried meat.

- **Dehydrated fish:** Fish is another source of protein for your dog, and it can also provide omega-3 fatty acids that are beneficial for your dog's skin, coat, and joints. You can dehydrate fish from various sources such as salmon, tuna, cod, sardine, etc. You can cut the fish into thin strips and dehydrate it at **145°F (63°C)** for **4 to 8 hours**, until it is dry and flaky. You can also season the fish with salt, pepper, and lemon juice if you like, but avoid bones that may pose a choking hazard. One pound (0.45 kg) of raw fish will yield about **4 ounces (113 g)** of dried fish.

- **Dehydrated fruits and vegetables:** Fruits and vegetables can provide vitamins, minerals, fiber, and antioxidants for your dog, and they can also add some variety and flavor to your dog's diet. You can dehydrate fruits and vegetables from various sources such as apple, banana, carrot, sweet potato, pumpkin, zucchini, etc. You can cut the fruits and vegetables into thin slices and dehydrate them at **135°F (57°C)** for **6 to 10 hours**, until they are crisp or chewy. You can also sprinkle some cinnamon or garlic powder if you like, but avoid fruits and vegetables that are toxic or high in sugar for dogs, such as grapes, raisins, onion, garlic, etc. One pound (0.45 kg) of raw fruits or vegetables will yield about **2 to 3 ounces (57 to 85 g)** of dried fruits or vegetables.

To make a balanced and complete diet for your dog, you need to combine the dehydrated food with other ingredients such as water, broth, eggs, yogurt, cheese, etc. You can also add some supplements such as vitamins, minerals, probiotics, etc. if needed. You should rehydrate the dehydrated food before feeding it to your dog, by adding water or broth and letting it soak for a few minutes. You should also consult your veterinarian before making any changes to your dog's diet, and monitor your dog's weight, appetite, energy, and stool quality.

Dehydrated treats
Meat

Chicken jerky: Cut boneless, skinless chicken breasts into thin slices with the grain. Dehydrate at **160°F (71°C)** for **4 to 8 hours**, until they are crispy and break easily. One pound (0.45 kg) of raw chicken will yield about **4 ounces (113 g)** of dried jerky. Chicken jerky is a good source of protein, vitamins, and minerals for dogs. It can also help keep their teeth clean and gums healthy.

Beef jerky: Cut lean beef into thin slices against the grain. Season with salt, pepper, garlic powder, and parsley if desired. Dehydrate at **155°F (68°C)** for **5 to 10 hours**, until they are dry and chewy. One pound (0.45 kg) of raw beef will yield about **4 ounces (113 g)** of dried jerky. Beef jerky is a good source of protein, iron, zinc, and B vitamins for dogs. It can also help support their muscle growth and immune system.

Turkey jerky: Cut lean turkey into thin slices with the grain. Season with salt, pepper, rosemary, and sage if desired. Dehydrate at **165°F (74°C)** for **6 to 12 hours**, until they are dry and chewy. One pound (0.45 kg) of raw turkey will yield about **4 ounces (113 g)** of dried jerky. Turkey jerky is a good source of protein, selenium, phosphorus, and tryptophan for dogs. It can also help promote their mood and sleep quality.

Lamb jerky: Cut lean lamb into thin slices against the grain. Season with salt, pepper, rosemary, and mint if desired. Dehydrate at **160°F (71°C)** for **4 to 8 hours**, until they are dry and chewy. One pound (0.45 kg) of raw lamb will yield about **4 ounces (113 g)** of dried jerky. Lamb jerky is a good source of protein, iron, zinc, and B vitamins for dogs. It can also help reduce inflammation and allergies in dogs.

Pork loin treats: Cut pork loin into thin slices against the grain. Season with salt, pepper, and garlic powder if desired. Dehydrate at **150°F (66°C)** for **6 to 10 hours**, until they are dry and chewy. One pound (0.45 kg) of raw pork loin will yield about **4 ounces (113 g)** of dried treats. Pork loin treats are a good source of protein, thiamine, and niacin for dogs. They can also help improve their energy and metabolism.

Venison jerky: Cut venison into thin slices against the grain. Season with salt, pepper, and thyme if desired. Dehydrate at **160°F (71°C)** for **4 to 8 hours**, until they are dry and chewy. One pound (0.45 kg) of raw venison will yield about **4 ounces (113 g)** of dried jerky. Venison jerky is a good source of protein, iron, and B vitamins for dogs. It can also help prevent food allergies and sensitivities in dogs.

Duck breast treats: Cut duck breast into thin slices with the grain. Dehydrate at **165°F (74°C) b 6 to 12 hours**, until they are dry and chewy. One pound (0.45 kg) of raw duck breast will yield about **4 ounces (113 g)** of dried treats. Duck breast treats are a good source of protein, iron, and selenium for dogs. They can also help support their immune system and thyroid function.

Offal

Liver treats: Buy liver in any protein you like, such as chicken, beef, lamb, or turkey. Slice into **1/8" to 3/8" (0.3 cm to 1 cm)** thick pieces. Dehydrate at **160-165°F (71-74°C)** for **10 to 12 hours**, until they are dry and crisp. One pound (0.45 kg) of raw liver will yield about **3 ounces (85 g)** of dried treats. Liver treats are a great source of iron, vitamin A, and B vitamins, and have a strong and savory flavor that dogs crave. They can be used as a training treat or a supplement.

Beef kidney treats: Rinse the beef kidneys and trim off any excess fat or connective tissue. Cut into **1/4" (0.6 cm)** thick pieces. Dehydrate at **155 (68°C)** for **6 to 8 hours**, until they are dry and crisp. One pound (0.45 kg) of raw beef kidney will yield about **3 ounces (85 g)** of dried treats. Beef kidney treats are a good source of protein, iron, and B vitamins, and have a meaty and smoky flavor that dogs love. They can be used as a snack or a supplement.

Turkey heart treats: Rinse the turkey hearts and trim off any excess fat or connective tissue. Cut into **1/4" (0.6 cm)** thick pieces. Dehydrate at **160°F (70°C)** for **8 to 12 hours**, until they are dry and chewy. One pound (0.45 kg) of raw turkey heart will yield about **4 ounces (113 g)** of dried treats. Turkey heart treats are a good source of protein, iron, and taurine, and have a meaty and chewy flavor that dogs love. They can be used as a snack or a meal topper.

Duck or Chicken gizzard treats: Rinse the duck gizzards and trim off any excess fat or connective tissue. Cut into **1/4" (0.6 cm)** thick pieces. Dehydrate at **160°F (70°C)** for **10 to 12 hour**s, until they are dry and chewy. One pound (0.45 kg) of raw duck gizzard will yield about 4 ounces (113 g) of dried treats. Duck gizzard treats are a good source of protein, iron, and zinc, and have a crunchy and savory flavor that dogs love. They can be used as a dental chew or a treat.

Pork spleen treats: Rinse the pork spleen and trim off any excess fat or connective tissue. Cut into **1/4" (0.6 cm)** thick pieces. Dehydrate at **155°F (68°C)** for **8 to 12 hours**, until they are dry and crisp. One pound (0.45 kg) of raw pork spleen will yield about **3 ounces (85 g)** of dried treats. Pork spleen treats are a good source of protein, iron, and vitamin C, and have a mild and crisp flavor that dogs like. They can be used as a treat or a supplement.

Lamb lung treats: Rinse the lamb lungs and trim off any excess fat or connective tissue. Cut into **1/4" (0.6 cm)** thick pieces. Dehydrate at **145°F (63°C)** for **10 to 12 hours**, until they are dry and flaky. One pound (0.45 kg) of raw lamb lung will yield about **3 ounces (85 g)** of dried treats. Lamb lung treats are a good source of protein and low in fat, and have a light and airy flavor that dogs like. They can be used as a treat or a supplement.

Salmon skin treats: Rinse the salmon skin and cut into **1/4" (0.6 cm)** wide strips. Dehydrate at **145°F (63°C)** for **4 to 8 hours**, until they are dry and crunchy. One pound (0.45 kg) of raw salmon skin will yield about **4 ounces (113 g)** of dried treats. Salmon skin treats are high in protein and omega-3 fatty acids, and have a fishy and crunchy flavor that dogs love. They can be used as a treat or a supplement.

Venison tripe treats: Rinse the venison tripe and cut into **1/4" (0.6 cm)** wide strips. Dehydrate at **165°F (74°C)** for **4 to 8 hours**, until they are dry and chewy. One pound (0.45 kg) of raw venison tripe will yield about **4 ounces (113 g)** of dried treats. Venison tripe treats are high in protein and low in fat, and have a chewy texture that dogs love. They can be used as a snack or a meal topper.

Chicken feet treat: Rinse the chicken feet and trim off any nails or excess skin. Cut into **1/4" (0.6 cm)** wide pieces. Dehydrate at **169°F (71°C)** for **4 to 8 hours**, until they are dry and crunchy. One pound (0.45 kg) of raw chicken feet will yield about **4 ounces (113 g)** of dried treats. Chicken feet treats are high in protein and glucosamine, and have a crunchy and cartilaginous flavor that dogs love. They can be used as a dental chew or a treat.

Beef tongue treats: Rinse the beef tongue and trim off any excess fat or connective tissue. Cut into **1/4" (0.6 cm)** thick pieces. Dehydrate at **150°F (65°C)** for **9 to 12 hours**, until they are dry and chewy. One pound (0.45 kg) of raw beef tongue will yield about **4 ounces (113 g)** of dried treats. Beef tongue treats are high in protein and low in fat, and have a meaty and chewy flavor that dogs love. They can be used as a snack or a meal topper.

Fish

Salmon jerky: Cut skinless salmon fillets into thin strips. Season with salt, pepper, and dill if desired. Dehydrate at **160°F (71°C)** for **5 to 9 hours**, until they are dry and flaky. One pound (0.45 kg) of raw salmon will yield about **4 ounces (113 g)** of dried jerky. Salmon jerky is high in protein and omega-3 fatty acids, which can help support your dog's skin, coat, and joint health.

Tuna jerky: Cut tuna steaks into thin strips. Season with salt, pepper, and parsley if desired. Dehydrate at **155°F (68°C)** for **6 to 10 hours**, until they are dry and flaky. One pound (0.45 kg) of raw tuna will yield about **4 ounces (113 g)** of dried jerky. Tuna jerky is high in protein and omega-3 fatty acids, which can help boost your dog's immune system and brain function.

Cod, Haddock or Pollock jerky: Cut cod, haddock or Pollock fillets into thin strips. Season with salt, pepper, and lemon juice if desired. Dehydrate at **150°F (66°C)** for **7 to 11 hours**, until they are dry and flaky. One pound (0.45 kg) of raw cod, haddock or Pollock will yield about

4 ounces (113 g) of dried jerky. Cod, haddock or Pollock jerky is high in protein and low in fat, which can help maintain your dog's muscle mass and weight.

Sardine treats: Rinse and drain canned sardines in water or oil. Cut into thin pieces. Dehydrate at **145°F (63°C)** for **5 to 9 hours**, until they are dry and crisp. One pound (0.45 kg) of canned sardines will yield about **4 ounces (113 g)** of dried treats. Sardine treats are high in protein and omega-3 fatty acids, which can help reduce inflammation and improve your dog's heart health.

Vegetable

Sweet potato chews: Wash sweet potatoes or yams and remove any green spots on the peel. Cut into thin pieces. Dehydrate at **125°F (52°C)** for **8 to 10 hours**, until they are bendy but not brittle. One pound (0.45 kg) of raw sweet potato will yield about **3 ounces (85 g)** of dried chews. Sweet potato chews are rich in fiber, vitamin A, and antioxidants, which can help support your dog's digestive and immune health.

Carrot chips: Scrub and peel carrots and cut into thin rounds. Dehydrate at **130°F (54°C)** for **8 to 12 hours**, until they are crisp. One pound (0.45 kg) of raw carrot will yield about **2 ounces (57 g)** of dried chips. Carrot chips are a good source of vitamin A, fiber, and beta-carotene, which can help improve your dog's vision and skin health.

Pumpkin treats: Scrub and peel a pumpkin and cut it into thin slices. Discard the seeds and pulp. Dehydrate at **125°F (52°C)** for **8 to 12 hours**, until they are crisp. One pound (0.45 kg) of raw pumpkin will yield about **2 ounces (57 g)** of dried treats. Pumpkin treats are a good source of vitamin A, fiber, and antioxidants, which can help regulate your dog's bowel movements and prevent diarrhea.

Zucchini chips: Rinse and slice zucchini into thin rounds. Sprinkle with a light dusting of garlic powder if desired. Dehydrate at **130°F (54°C)** for **8 to 12 hours**, until they are crisp. One pound (0.45 kg) of raw zucchini will yield about **2 ounces (57 g)** of dried chips. Zucchini chips are a good source of vitamin A, vitamin C, fiber, and antioxidants, which can help protect your dog's cells from oxidative stress and inflammation.

Beet treats: Rinse and peel beets and cut them into thin pieces. Dehydrate at **130°F (54°C)** for **7 to 11 hours**, until they are chewy. One pound (0.45 kg) of raw beets will yield about **3 ounces (85 g)** of dried treats. Beet treats are a good source of vitamin C, iron, and folate, which can help boost your dog's immune system and blood health.

Fruity

Banana chips: Peel and cut ripe bananas into thin rounds. Soak them in lemon juice to prevent browning. Dehydrate at **125°F (52°C)** for **8 to 12 hours**, until they are crunchy. One pound (0.45 kg) of raw banana will yield about **3 ounces (85 g)** of dried chips. Banana chips are a good source of potassium, vitamin C, and fiber, which can help support your dog's heart, immune, and digestive health.

Peanut butter banana chips: Peel and cut ripe bananas into thin rounds. Coat them with peanut butter (make sure it does not contain xylitol, which is toxic to dogs). Dehydrate at **125°F (52°C)** for **8 to 12 hours**, until they are crunchy. One pound (0.45 kg) of raw banana will yield about 3 ounces (85 g) of dried chips. Peanut butter banana chips are a good source of protein, healthy fats, and antioxidants, which can help improve your dog's energy, skin, and coat health.

Apple rings: Wash and core apples and cut them into thin rings. Sprinkle with a light dusting of cinnamon if desired. Dehydrate at **130°F (54°C)** for **7 to 9 hours**, until they are crisp. One pound (0.45 kg) of raw apple will yield about **2 ounces (57 g)** of dried rings. Apple rings are a good source of vitamin C, fiber, and phytochemicals, which can help protect your dog's cells from oxidative damage and inflammation. They have a sweet and tangy flavor that dogs like. They can be used as a snack or a kibble enhancer.

Mango treats: Peel and cut ripe mangoes into thin pieces. Dehydrate at **130°F (54°C)** for **7 to 11 hours**, until they are chewy. One pound (0.45 kg) of raw mango will yield about **3 ounces (85 g)** of dried treats. Mango treats are a good source of vitamin A, vitamin C, and beta-carotene, which can help support your dog's vision, skin, and immune health.

Pineapple treats: Peel and core pineapple and cut into thin pieces. Dehydrate at **130°F (54°C)** for **7 to 11 hours**, until they are chewy. One pound (0.45 kg) of raw pineapple will yield about **3 ounces (85 g)** of dried treats. Pineapple treats are a good source of vitamin C, manganese, and bromelain, which can help boost your dog's immune system, bone health, and digestion.

Strawberry treats: Wash and hull strawberries and slice into 1/4" (0.6 cm) thick pieces. Dehydrate at **135°F (57°C)** for **6 to 10 hours**, until they are chewy. One pound (0.45 kg) of raw strawberries will yield about 3 ounces (85 g) of dried treats. Strawberry treats are a good source of vitamin C, fiber, and antioxidants, which can help prevent infections and diseases in your dog.

Cats

Dehydrated food for cats has several advantages over other types of food, such as being easier to store and transport, having a longer shelf life, and preserving the natural nutrients and flavors of the food. However, dehydrated food for cats should not be the main food for your cat, but rather a supplement or a treat. This is because dehydrated food for cats does not provide enough moisture for your cat, which can lead to dehydration and urinary problems. Cats need about 60 to 70 ml of water per kilogram of body weight per day, and they usually get most of their water intake from their food. Therefore, if you feed your cat dehydrated food, you need to make sure they have access to fresh water at all times and also feed them wet food or raw food to balance their hydration levels. Dehydrated food for cats can be good for your cat if you use it as a treat or a topper for their regular food, as it can provide them with extra protein, vitamins, minerals, and antioxidants, as well as stimulate their appetite and taste buds. Dehydrated food for cats can also be beneficial for cats with food allergies or sensitivities, as it often contains limited ingredients and novel protein sources, such as rabbit, duck, or lamb. Dehydrated food for cats can also help with dental health and weight management, as it can reduce plaque and tartar buildup, and prevent overeating and obesity. Dehydrated food for cats can be a great way to feed your cat a raw diet without the hassle of preparing and storing raw food. However, you need to be careful about the quality and safety of dehydrated food for cats, as some products may contain harmful bacteria. You should also consult your veterinarian before switching your cat to a dehydrated food diet, as they can advise you on the best options and amounts for your cat's individual needs.

Lean Meats: Chicken, turkey, beef, salmon. Remove skin/bones and cut into thin strips, about ⅛ **inch (0.32 cm) thick and 2 inch (5.08 cm) long**. Place the strips on the dehydrator rack, leaving some space between them. Dehydrate for **6 to 8 hours at 165°F (74°C)** or until dry and brittle. You will get about **0.25 pounds (113 g)** of dried treats from 1 pound (454 g) of raw meat. These treats are good for your cat because they are high in protein and low in fat, which helps maintain a healthy weight and muscle mass.

Fish: (All pre-cooked) tuna, salmon, whitefish. Flake before dehydrating. Spread the flakes evenly on a parchment paper-lined dehydrator tray. Dehydrate for **4 to 6 hours** at **140°F (60°C)** or until dry and flaky. You will get about **0.1 pounds (45 g)** of dried treats from 1 pound (454 g) of cooked fish. These treats are good for your cat because they are high in omega-3 fatty acids, which support healthy skin and coat, as well as brain and heart health.

Eggs: Hard-boil an egg, slice it thinly, and dehydrate it into crunchy bits. Place the slices on the dehydrator rack, leaving some space between them. Dehydrate for **4 to 6 hours** at **145°F**

(63°C) or until dry and crisp. You will get about **0.05 pounds (23 g)** of dried treats from 1 pound (454 g) of eggs. These treats are good for your cat because they are high in protein and fat, which provide energy and support growth and development.

Cheese: Low-fat cheeses like cheddar, Swiss, and mozzarella cut into small cubes, about ¼ **inch (0.64 cm)** on each side. Place the cubes on the dehydrator rack, leaving some space between them. Dehydrate for **8 to 10 hours** at **125°F (52°C)** or until dry and hard. You will get about **0.9 pounds (408 g)** of dried treats from 1 pound (454 g) of cheese. These treats are good for your cat because they are high in calcium and phosphorus, which support strong bones and teeth, as well as protein and fat, which provide energy and support growth and development.

Fruits: Apples, bananas, blueberries, cranberries, pineapple. Cut small or puree before dehydrating. Spread the fruit pieces or puree evenly on a parchment paper-lined dehydrator tray. Dehydrate for **8 to 10 hours** at **135°F (57°C)** or until dry and chewy. You will get about **0.1 pounds (45 g)** of dried treats from 1 pound (454 g) of fresh fruit. These treats are good for your cat because they are high in antioxidants, vitamins, and minerals, which support a healthy immune system and prevent oxidative stress and inflammation.

Vegetables: Green beans, sweet potato, pumpkin, carrots. Slice thinly or grate before dehydrating. Spread the vegetable pieces or shreds evenly on a parchment paper-lined dehydrator tray. Dehydrate for **8 to 10 hours** at **135°F (57°C)** or until dry and crunchy. You will get about 0.1 pounds (45 g) of dried treats from 1 pound (454 g) of fresh vegetables. These treats are good for your cat because they are high in fiber, vitamins, and minerals, which support a healthy digestive system and prevent constipation and diarrhea.

Grains: Oats, barley, rice. Cook first, then dehydrate into crunchy cereals. Spread the cooked grains evenly on a parchment paper-lined dehydrator tray. Dehydrate for **8 to 10 hours** at **125°F (52°C)** or until dry and crisp. You will get about **0.8 pounds (363 g)** of dried treats from 1 pound (454 g) of cooked grains. These treats are good for your cat because they are high in carbohydrates, which provide energy and support a healthy metabolism, as well as fiber, which supports a healthy digestive system and prevents constipation and diarrhea.

Herbs: Catnip, cat grass. Dehydrate fresh leaves. Place the leaves on the dehydrator rack, leaving some space between them. Dehydrate for **2 to 4 hours** at **95°F (35°C)** or until dry and crumbly. You will get about **0.02 pounds (9 g)** of dried treats from 1 pound (454 g) of fresh herbs. These treats are good for your cat because they are high in phytochemicals, which have various effects on your cat's behavior and mood, such as stimulating, relaxing, or soothing.

When you make dehydrated food for your cat, you should consider the following factors:

The quality and safety of the ingredients: You should use fresh, raw, human-grade ingredients that are free of hormones, antibiotics, pesticides, and other harmful substances. You should also wash and trim the ingredients before dehydrating them, and avoid using any seasonings, spices, or additives that may be toxic or harmful to your cat.

The storage and shelf life of the dehydrated food: You should store the dehydrated food in airtight containers or bags, and keep them in a cool, dry, and dark place. You should also label the containers or bags with the date of dehydration and the type of food. You should use the dehydrated food within 6 months to 1 year, depending on the type of food and the storage conditions. You should also check the dehydrated food for any signs of mold, spoilage, or insect infestation before feeding it to your cat.

The rehydration and serving of the dehydrated food: You should rehydrate the dehydrated food before feeding it to your cat, as dehydrated food can cause dehydration and urinary problems if fed dry. You should use warm water to rehydrate the dehydrated food and follow the instructions of the recipe or the product. You should also adjust the amount of water and the rehydration time according to your cat's preference and the texture of the food. You should serve the rehydrated food within 30 minutes of rehydration, and discard any leftovers. You should also provide fresh water for your cat at all times, and monitor your cat's hydration level and urine output.

For your notes

Made in United States
Troutdale, OR
01/08/2025

27732613R00086